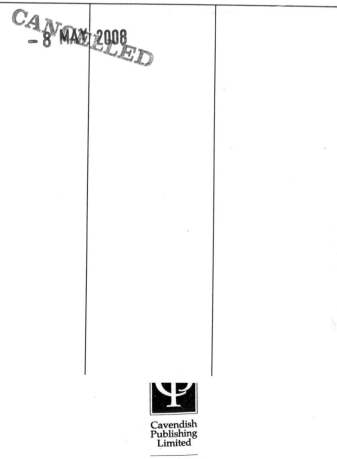
20/7/06

Cavendish
Publishing
Limited

London • Sydney • Portland, Oregon

MEDIATION:
A PRACTICAL GUIDE

Allan J Stitt

Cavendish
Publishing
Limited

London • Sydney • Portland, Oregon

First published in Great Britain 2004 by
Cavendish Publishing Limited, The Glass House,
Wharton Street, London WC1X 9PX, United Kingdom
Telephone: + 44 (0)20 7278 8000   Facsimile: + 44 (0)20 7278 8080
Email: info@cavendishpublishing.com
Website: www.cavendishpublishing.com

Published in the United States by Cavendish Publishing
c/o International Specialized Book Services,
5824 NE Hassalo Street, Portland,
Oregon 97213-3644, USA

Published in Australia by Cavendish Publishing (Australia) Pty Ltd
45 Beach Street, Coogee, NSW 2034, Australia
Telephone: + 61 (2)9664 0909   Facsimile: + 61 (2)9664 5420
Email: info@cavendishpublishing.com.au
Website: www.cavendishpublishing.com.au

British Library Cataloguing in Publication Data
Stitt, Allan, 1961–
Mediation: a practical guide
1 Dispute resolution (Law) 2 Mediation
I Title
347'.09

Library of Congress Cataloguing in Publication Data
Data available

ISBN 1-85941-844-9

3 5 7 9 10 8 6 4 2

Printed and bound in Great Britain

In memory of my grandparents, Myers and Belle Stitt and Leon and Elsie Pape

FOREWORD BY LORD GOFF OF CHIEVELEY

Allan Stitt is an outstanding exponent of the art and he himself is a skilled and experienced mediator, but he is also a born teacher who gives courses on mediation, securely founded on his practical experience and enlivened by his wicked sense of humour. I myself have attended one of these courses with much enjoyment and to my great profit.

The present book is a version designed for the UK market of Allan Stitt's Canadian book *Mediating Commercial Disputes*, with which I am familiar and for which I entertain great respect. I have had the opportunity of reading the present book in proof, and I have seen for myself the various alterations which have been made to acclimatise the book for the UK market. They are all sensible and mostly very simple; they do nothing to detract from the admirable text of the Canadian book. Indeed, the present book retains all the virtues of the Canadian book, including the admirable 'Tips for Lawyers' and 'Tips for Mediators', and the vivid illustrations headed 'It Happened at Mediation'. I am therefore well equipped to recommend the present book, which I gladly do most warmly.

As mediation becomes more and more highly regarded as a method of dispute resolution, so books of the quality and practical utility of the present book become more and more necessary for the guidance of aspiring mediators, and useful too for mediators who already have experience in practice. I believe that I speak for mediators in this country when I say that we are most fortunate to be able to place this book on our bookshelves, alongside the books already there, ready to give us authoritative guidance on the conduct of mediations and on the solution of problems that may arise in the course of our work.

Robert Goff
September 2003

FOREWORD BY SIR BRIAN NEILL

Allan Stitt has written a book of outstanding merit that will be of great value to both his primary audiences – (a) the lawyers who participate in mediations; and (b) the mediators themselves. The tips at the end of each chapter are full of wise advice. Furthermore, I believe that all who practise in this field will benefit from studying Allan Stitt's own experiences as demonstrated in his series of 'It Happened at Mediation'. But perhaps the most valuable lesson to be learned from this book is the need for the mediator to be flexible and imaginative. The chapters entitled 'Issues' and 'Brainstorming Options', for example, show Allan Stitt's gift for perceptive analysis and creative thinking. He is a master of his craft.

Sir Brian Neill

ACKNOWLEDGMENTS

I am extremely fortunate to live with and work with kind and helpful people who support me, put up with my idiosyncrasies, and give me guidance. My partners, Frank Handy and Lisa Feld, not only encouraged me to write this book, but also covered for me to give me the time I needed when my deadline approached and I still had work to do. Others at the Stitt Feld Handy Group continually challenge me, give me ideas, and seem always to have solutions to even the most challenging problems.

I wish I were the kind of writer who, like Shakespeare, could write a first draft and have it be my final draft. Unfortunately, I'm not nearly that good. A lot of people reviewed earlier drafts of this book and gave me extremely helpful comments that I have incorporated into the final draft. Frank Handy, Elinor Whitmore, Mike Wadsworth, Steve Lancken and Michael Gibson all provided feedback and suggestions, and all made the book better. In addition, Paul Godin assisted me with research and put together the bibliography. Lisa Feld, Roger Beaudry, Peter Dreyer and Nancy Lamarche also contributed ideas.

I learn from every mediation that I conduct. Fortunately, the vast majority of people for whom I have mediated have given me permission to write about the details of their mediations, on an anonymous basis, for educational purposes. Without their consent, I could not have provided the examples that I have used in this book to help clarify the ideas I have presented.

Finally, I want to thank my family. My parents-in-law, Linda and Larry Levenstein, have always supported my endeavours. My parents, Bert and Barbara, have taught me that it is better to work through issues than to fight. They have shown me how positive reinforcement and support can help people work through difficult issues. It is from watching them that I learned many of my mediation skills. My kids, Jason, Melanie and Lindsay are my inspiration. My children are naturally inquisitive, intuitive and open to new ideas, all essential skills for mediators and participants in mediation. They constantly remind me of the importance of asking why and of not making assumptions. Most importantly, I want to thank my wife, Sari. She is my rock, my best friend and my strongest supporter. She gets none of the credit, and deserves it all. She has had to put up with my writing a book during our vacations, my mediations that go late and cause me to miss family dinners, and my complaining about all that I have to do. Through it all, she keeps supporting me and inspires me to do my best. Thank you.

CONTENTS

INTRODUCTION

Before we were civilised, we resolved conflict by force. The person with the greater ability to use force (the person with power) was the winner and the weaker person was the loser. Clearly, however, force was not always the best way to resolve conflict and a fair result was not always achieved when people took matters into their own hands. So society devised another approach to resolving conflict: litigation.

Throughout the last couple of centuries, people who could not resolve disputes on their own went to court to ask a judge to impose a solution. Judges, who were seen as the best people in society to come up with solutions to complex problems, made decisions as best they could, applying the law to the facts, and trying to balance the interests of the individual with the interests of society.

Litigation was perceived to be superior to self-help in resolving disputes because it had procedural safeguards and rules that increased the likelihood that the result would be just. That being said, until relatively recently, it was generally used only as a last resort. Before going to court, people would usually try to resolve conflict themselves, or go to a respected person in society to get advice or guidance.

Recently, however, litigation has become the automatic first step for people in dispute. Litigation has also been gradually losing its claim as being the best way to resolve conflict, in part because the procedural safeguards that are so important have made it necessary to create cumbersome processes that do not always produce the best and most efficient outcome.

So society is looking for new and innovative methods to deal with people in dispute, or a return to less litigious ways to resolve conflict. We want results that are fair, but we do not want cumbersome and time consuming processes. We therefore look back to a time when we turned to respected and creative people who had the skills to help us resolve conflict, and that look back is leading us to mediation.

While mediation in various forms has been around for many years, it is now being reborn as a more effective stage in the evolution of how we, as a society, resolve conflict.

I have written this book for people who are interested in mediation and are interested in exploring new and innovative ways to resolve conflict. That being said, I believe that I have two primary audiences. The first is lawyers who participate in mediations and want a guide so that they can be effective advocates. The second is people who want to acquire mediation skills to help others resolve conflict. I have tried to present and discuss the issues that these audiences might want to consider both before and during a mediation.

In the first part of the book, I present some of these issues, focusing particularly on the ones that mediation participants will want to consider before the start of the mediation. I then move to the mediation process generally and describe it, mixing the discussion with examples of mediations in which I have participated. I then identify some of the obstacles that can prevent parties from reaching agreement at mediation and I provide some thoughts on how to overcome the obstacles.

At the end of each chapter, there is a section called 'Tips for Lawyers'. The 'Tips for Lawyers' are concrete suggestions that lawyers may choose to use strategically in mediations to get a better deal for their clients. In these sections, I have attempted to summarise some of the key points that I have raised in the chapter and put them in a form that lawyers can use in their preparation for mediations. I have also tried to create the Tips as stand-alone advice that lawyers can refer to as a refresher for the topics in that chapter.

Similarly, there is a section at the end of each chapter called 'Tips for Mediators'. These sections are designed for people who are interested in learning the tools they need to mediate and help others deal with conflict. Like the 'Tips for Lawyers', the 'Tips for Mediators' can be used as reminders of the points raised in each chapter or can stand alone.

As mentioned above, I have included numerous examples from cases that I have mediated to enliven points. My hope is that the examples will bring to life the ideas that are presented. I have tried to make each example brief and to the point, and have tried to avoid making the example sound like a 'war story'. Most examples have the heading 'It Happened at Mediation' and are in shaded boxes. While all of the facts used in the examples are based on actual cases, I have not used real names and, in some of the cases, I have slightly altered some facts to protect the confidentiality of the mediations and the anonymity of the disputants. In some examples I have combined the facts of two cases I have mediated in one example.

I have tried to keep in mind throughout that there is no one right way to mediate and, as a result, there is no way that is necessarily wrong. I have done my best to present ideas that I hope will be helpful to the reader, and I have tried, where appropriate, to indicate where there is a difference of opinion among those who consider a particular issue.

The first issue around which there is some difference of opinion is the best style for a mediator to adopt. This is where I will begin.

CHAPTER 1

MEDIATOR STYLES

1.1   WHAT IS MEDIATION?

Mediation is, simply, facilitated negotiation. A mediator attempts to help people negotiate more effectively and efficiently than they could on their own. The mediator helps the disputants[1] to find solutions to their conflict that make more sense to them than continuing with their dispute. The mediator helps them search for common ground and find creative yet realistic ways to resolve their issues.

Rule number one for the mediator is, above all, do no harm.[2] A mediator should make sure that disputants do not leave the mediation in worse shape than when they arrived.

Rule number two is that, other than rule number one, there are no absolute rules. There are many ways for a mediator to help people negotiate and any method may be appropriate, depending on the circumstances. Mediators will try different techniques, be creative and use innovative approaches to try to help disputants find solutions to their problems.

1.2   A FAIR RESULT

Do we want mediators to move disputants toward a 'fair' solution? The obvious answer would appear to be yes.

Suppose Company A has breached a contract by failing to supply goods on time as promised, and as a result Company B has suffered £1 million in damages. Company A has come up with all kinds of excuses, arguing that Company B caused delays and did not want to accommodate by accepting orders after 5:00 pm. Suppose the mediator thinks Company A's excuses are weak, and would probably not be accepted by a judge. Shouldn't the mediator help lead the disputants to a solution whereby Company A appropriately compensates Company B? That seems fair and it seems obvious that a good mediator would push the disputants to reach a fair solution. But is that what a good mediator would do?

What is a fair solution? Who should decide what is fair? Should Company A have to pay Company B £1 million? How does a mediator know for sure what a court would do? Would a court even necessarily deliver a fair result? What about the risk that the mediator is wrong about what a court would do? After all, no one can predict with certainty what a court will do and a court may accept one of Company A's excuses. Should a mediator's opinion of what is fair be determinative? Not always.

---

1   I have used the term 'disputants' throughout the book to refer to the parties involved in the conflict.
2   I first heard this rule from my friend, Brian H Wheatley of ADR Chambers.

For many disputes, the mediator should not focus on what he or she believes is fair; instead, the mediator should help the disputants to see whether they can come up with a solution that they both want to accept, regardless of the mediator's subjective sense of fairness. The mediator's concept of what is fair may not be the same as the disputants' and it is the disputants who will have to live with the result, not the mediator. Disputants may want a mediator who will focus on their underlying interests and facilitate the discussion in a way that helps them come to their own conclusions and solutions. This type of mediator is known as 'facilitative'.

On the other hand, depending on the situation, the nature of the dispute and the identity of the mediator, the disputants may want someone who directs them toward a particular result. Sometimes disputants want mediators who will evaluate the arguments raised by them and try to persuade them about what is fair. This type of mediator is known as 'evaluative'.

Evaluative mediators are sometimes referred to as 'rights-based' because it is assumed that these mediators focus on the disputants' legal rights. The truth is that the term 'rights-based' is probably deceptive, as facilitative mediators also usually spend time focusing on legal rights and the consequences of not reaching agreement.

Facilitative mediators are sometimes referred to as 'interest-based' because these mediators focus on the disputants' underlying interests or goals. Once again, the term may be deceptive, as many evaluative mediators also try to focus on disputants' interests and needs when evaluating the dispute and determining what is fair.

There are some important distinctions in the way that facilitative and evaluative mediators manage the mediation process.

1.3   EVALUATION MEDIATION

Evaluative mediators rely on their expertise and experience to assess situations and reach conclusions about the relative merits of the arguments that are being presented to them. Evaluative mediators are often retired judges or politicians, senior lawyers or accountants, or people who are respected and have a lot of experience in a particular field such as computers, engineering, accounting or sports.

In an evaluative mediation, the role of the disputants (and their lawyers) is to present persuasive arguments that will convince the mediator that the disputant has a strong case and will win if the matter goes to trial. Presentations to the mediator are in the form of legal arguments, usually made by a lawyer. The process is similar to a court process, without the formality, and that is why some refer to evaluative mediation as non-binding arbitration. Evaluative mediation is non-binding in the sense that the disputants need not accept the mediator's evaluation of the merits of the case. Disputants can conclude, as they often do, that the mediator has misconstrued the facts, misapplied the law or just missed the point, and that the disputants will be better off going to court and taking their chances with a judge.

If the disputants do not agree with the evaluative mediator's assessment, the mediator may attempt to persuade them of the accuracy of the assessment. Some evaluative mediators try to bully the disputants into agreeing. Evaluative mediation is therefore sometimes referred to as 'muscle mediation'.

Evaluative mediation is frowned upon by some mediators who believe that it is not 'true' mediation, as the mediator does not facilitate, but rather judges. They argue that it should not be considered mediation; it should be called non-binding judging or non-binding arbitration. Others believe, however, that evaluative mediation serves an important role for those in conflict, as it provides disputants with an opportunity to receive an unbiased evaluation of their case without the expense of a trial. It also moves the mediation from a somewhat subjective process to a more objective one, focusing on the mediator's assessment and standard of fairness.

People sometimes assume that if they have a strong case, and if they are in the right, then evaluative mediation will better serve them than facilitative mediation. They believe that the mediator will undoubtedly agree with them, that the other side will be told they have a weak case, and that the other side will accept the mediator's assessment. Unfortunately, evaluative mediation is no more predictable than a trial. The evaluative mediator may not agree with the side that believes it has a strong case. Disputants in evaluative mediation take the risk that the mediator will not agree with their assessment of the strength of their case and, as a result, the other side may be less likely to reach an amicable resolution to the conflict than it was before the mediation.

Even if the evaluative mediator agrees that one side's case is strong, the other disputant may also believe that he or she has a strong case and may not be open to being persuaded by the mediator's views. The other side may believe that he or she is better off going to trial, hoping to find a judge who is more sympathetic to his or her argument than the mediator was. That does not mean, however, that evaluative mediation is never appropriate. For example, a lawyer may prefer an evaluative approach to a facilitative one if the lawyer believes that his or her own client is being unrealistic and perhaps obstreperous. Evaluative mediation may produce an opinion from the mediator that supports the lawyer's assessment, in which case the client may be persuaded to make concessions that he or she would not otherwise be prepared to make. Alternatively, the mediator may agree with the client's assessment and the lawyer may need to re-evaluate his or her assessment of the case.

Another situation in which evaluative mediation may be appropriate is a case where the dispute is a purely legal one. The disputants may decide that the opinion of a retired judge is as valid as the opinion of a sitting judge. They may decide to avoid the cost of litigation or arbitration and have an evaluative mediator provide an opinion based on brief presentations made at mediation, so that they will be better able to assess how a court would decide on the legal issue before it.

Evaluative mediation may also be appropriate where disputants have a technical dispute and need the opinion of a technical person in order to resolve the dispute. They may find someone to mediate whose opinion they both respect and may find persuasive.

1.4 FACILITATIVE MEDIATION

In a facilitative mediation, the mediator facilitates the discussion and the negotiation in an attempt to help the disputants find a solution that is acceptable to both (or all) of them. The mediator helps the disputants explore the options to determine whether there is an option that appeals to them. The mediator facilitates the discussion even when the mediator believes that the option being discussed is unfair.

The disputants and lawyers all play an active role in the process, though they try to persuade each other, not the mediator. The mediator's perception of what is right and what is fair will not play a major role in the process.

Facilitative mediators are experts in the process of negotiation and not necessarily the substance of what is being discussed (though they usually have some familiarity with it). The value that they bring to the mediation is negotiation expertise, helping disputants overcome obstacles in negotiation that they may not be able to overcome themselves.

Just because a mediation is facilitative does not mean that the mediator will not discuss with the disputants the strengths and weaknesses of their cases, attempt to determine the likelihood that each side will prevail at trial, and even suggest which arguments the mediator finds persuasive. What differentiates facilitative from evaluative mediation is that a facilitative mediator tries to enable the disputants to reach consensus on what they think is a fair outcome, while an evaluative mediator tries to lead the disputants to his or her own assessment of what is fair.

Which types of disputes are appropriate for facilitative mediation? It is difficult to predict when facilitative mediation will and will not lead to a settlement. Senior lawyers often say that the dispute in which they are acting is 'not ripe for mediation' or that the disputants are 'too intransigent' for the mediation to result in resolution. Far more often than not, these cases settle. The right question may not be, therefore, 'When is facilitative mediation appropriate?', but rather, 'Is facilitative mediation ever inappropriate?'.

Facilitative mediation can almost always be an appropriate way to proceed as it provides the disputants with an opportunity to talk, and possibly to settle their dispute. That being said, there are situations in which facilitative mediation is particularly appropriate.

Some disputants believe that they need to posture in order to cause the other side to make concessions. After each side takes a position on the issues, each disputant finds that the other does not agree with that position. Negotiations then take the form of the disputants attempting to persuade each other of the strength of their positions.

A facilitative mediator can step into the middle of the negotiation and establish a process that changes the focus of the discussion away from the positions and the problems, toward possible solutions. The mediator is neutral and espouses no bias toward the disputants. Consequently, he or she can assist the disputants to communicate through the mediator in a way that they cannot do by themselves. Therefore, when disputants have taken entrenched positions, facilitative mediation may be particularly appropriate.

The disputants may have confidential information that they do not want to disclose to the other side. The information may, however, if known, provide an important clue to a possible settlement. In a facilitative mediation, the disputants can confide in the mediator and ask that he or she keep the information confidential. Armed with such knowledge, the mediator may be able to structure the discussion so that settlement options that the mediator thinks may be workable are explored, while not disclosing anything confidential. Facilitative mediation may be particularly appropriate, therefore, for cases in which disputants have confidential information.

People have needs and interests that they try to meet by advocating positions. A primary role of a facilitative mediator is to uncover these underlying interests and try to help the disputants find a solution through which their interests are met.

Facilitative mediation may therefore be particularly appropriate for cases in which there are opportunities to come up with creative solutions that are not necessarily tied to the disputants' positions.

1.5   FACILITATIVE VERSUS EVALUATIVE MEDIATION

People tend to compartmentalise and give labels. At the end of the day, though, it doesn't really matter what label is placed on the mediation; what matters is that the mediator selected has the skill to maximise the disputants' opportunity to negotiate a resolution to their dispute. What also matters is that the disputants (or their lawyers) ask questions to find out the mediator's style before the mediator is selected so that there are no surprises at the mediation.

Throughout most of this book, I will focus on the mediator who uses a facilitative approach, helping disputants find a solution that they (not the mediator) believe is fair. This does not mean that the mediator does not discuss with the disputants the strengths and weaknesses of their arguments. In the right circumstances, the mediator may even play an evaluative role, suggesting what he or she believes is fair, to help disputants overcome an obstacle.

In an attempt to structure mediations that make sense for people who have ongoing relationships, some organisations design dispute resolution systems that help them find the most appropriate processes to resolve conflict. The attempt to set up appropriate processes has resulted in the recent growth of Alternative Dispute Resolution Systems Design.[3]

1.6   TRANSFORMATIVE MEDIATION

A third approach to mediation, called transformative, has recently been more clearly defined in mediation theory. It is closer to a facilitative than an evaluative approach. A transformative mediator is concerned with facilitating so that the disputants learn more about themselves, and learn a process that will help them resolve future conflict. In a transformative mediation, the process of trying to reach a result is as important as the result itself, and the dispute is the vehicle by which the disputants enter the process. A significant amount of the mediation focuses on the relationship between the disputants. Caucuses (or private meetings) are rare and the mediator spends a significant amount of time facilitating communication between or among disputants. Transformative mediations can take significantly longer than evaluative or facilitative mediations.

Transformative mediations are therefore most appropriate in situations where the disputants anticipate that they will have a number of disputes with each other in the future and need to learn a process that will help them resolve the disputes as they arise.

---

3   For a complete discussion of how organisations can set up systems to deal with conflict, see Stitt, AJ, *Alternative Dispute Resolution for Organisations: How to Design a System for Effective Conflict Resolution*, 1998, Toronto: John Wiley & Sons, Canada.

Tips for Lawyers

- Find out before a mediation what approach your mediator uses in mediation. Is the mediator evaluative, facilitative or transformative?

- If your clients feel strongly about the principle of their case and believe that a judge would side with them, and if you believe that your clients may not be realistic about their chances of success at trial, you may want to find an evaluative mediator. You may need the authority of a senior person with credibility who can give your clients an objective and realistic assessment of the case and will work to persuade you and your clients.

- If there is a dispute about a point of law or a technical issue and both sides agree that a determination of the legal issue will result in a fair resolution, it may make sense for an evaluative mediator to hear the issue and give an opinion. You will want to choose a mediator with the experience and the substantive expertise to give an impartial opinion that the disputants will seriously consider.

- The evaluative mediator will not necessarily agree with your assessment of the case, even if you believe you have a strong argument. Mediators are just as likely to surprise as judges are, and mediators have less information on which to base an opinion. Select an evaluative mediator only if you are prepared to accept the risk that the mediator may have an opinion that does not favour you.

- For most cases, you will want to select a mediator who is skilled at facilitating communication, bringing out the issues and controlling the process. You will want a mediator who can help you search for the best solution for you, even if that is a creative one and not based on what a court might (or even could) do. This does not mean that you should be afraid to ask the mediator to discuss with you the strengths and weaknesses of your arguments, nor should you be afraid to ask the mediator to give his or her opinion.

- If you are dealing with a dispute in which you anticipate that the disputants will have a number of ongoing disputes to deal with (such as an employment situation), you may consider transformative mediators who can help your clients not only solve their problem, but also find a way to deal civilly with each other in the future.

- If you are assisting an organisation to resolve internal disputes among staff, consider whether it would be valuable for the organisation to retain a consultant with the appropriate expertise to help in the design of an ADR system.

Tips for Mediators

- You must choose your own style of mediation. This does not mean you need a label for your approach, such as evaluative, facilitative or transformative. You should choose to be an effective mediator, and that may mean being able to facilitate discussion and, in some cases, give assessments of arguments, so long as you and all disputants clearly understand your role and the process.

CHAPTER 2

WHY MEDIATE?

2.1   IS MEDIATION WORTHWHILE?

Mediation cannot guarantee a settlement, and yet it will take time and cost disputants money. Even if the case does settle at mediation, it may have settled in any event; after all, the vast majority of cases settle without mediation. Mediation may prevent precedents from being set so the law may not develop as it otherwise would have. It is private so the public cannot find out whether the process and the outcome were fair. It can be abused by people who have power to take advantage of those who do not. It may unnecessarily open wounds. When mediation is conducted early in the litigation process, disputants are being asked to assess their cases and make decisions with limited facts; they need information to make proper and informed decisions. With all of these concerns and reasons not to mediate, why bother?

Let's examine the concerns raised above. The first is that mediation cannot guarantee settlement, yet it takes time and costs disputants money. Mediation would be a worthwhile process, however, if a significant number of cases settle at mediation or shortly thereafter.

Do a significant percentage of cases settle at mediation? Statistics suggest they do. For cases that voluntarily go to mediation, upward of 70–80% settle.[1] Even for mediations that are mandatory, where disputants are required to mediate as part of the litigation process, more than 40% of cases settle at mediation or within 10 days of the mediation.[2]

Mediations are almost always completed in a day, often in half a day, as compared with the years it can take to resolve a case at trial from the time of the Particulars of Claim to the time of decision by a judge.

But would these cases have settled anyway? Is mediation just an unnecessary added step in the process? It is true that most of those cases that settle at mediation would have settled in any event, but at a later date. Statistics suggest that cases that go to mediation settle sooner than cases that do not go to mediation, even where the mediation is mandatory.[3]

Where cases do not settle at mediation, there are still a number of benefits to having a mediation. For example, disputants may set the groundwork for a future settlement by discussing the issues and possible outcomes at mediation. In fact, cases that have gone through a mediation and not settled are more likely to settle earlier than cases that have not gone through that process.[4]

---

1   See, eg, Gillie, MS, 'Voluntary mediation' (1990) 26 Trial No 10, p 58.
2   See, eg, 'Ontario Mandatory Mediation Program Status Report', for the period ending 1 June 2002: Altobelli, Tom, 'NSW Supreme Court makes mediation mandatory' (2000) 3(3) ADR 43.
3   Hann, RG and Baa, C, *Evaluation of the Ontario Mandatory Mediation Program (Rule 24.1): Final Report – The First 23 Months*, 2001, Ottawa: Queen's Printer.
4   *Ibid.*

Further, the issues may be narrowed or the disputants may establish a schedule to save time and money. In addition, because disputants are in a room where they must listen to each other, they may gain an understanding of each other's views and perspectives, thus reducing the damage to the relationship that is inevitably caused by the litigation process.

Does mediation prevent precedents from being set and thereby prevent law from being developed? Probably not. Most cases settle with or without mediation and cases that would not have settled without mediation are unlikely to settle in mediation. Even if they do settle and would not have otherwise, can we really say that settlement is a bad thing? If disputants decide they are better off settling than going to trial, should we design a system that discourages settlement and encourages them to spend their money and go to trial? I think not. If we should discourage settlement through mediation, we should also discourage negotiations that might resolve disputes. After all, they too will prevent precedents from being set.

There may be times where a litigant has an interest in setting a precedent for his or her own benefit (as opposed to the public interest), and that may be a reason why mediation (and negotiation) may not be beneficial. This issue will be discussed in more detail later in this chapter.

Mediation is a private process and the public does not usually learn about either the process or the outcome. The courts, on the other hand, are public and open. Is the private nature of mediation necessarily bad? Perhaps it is not always a good thing to ask disputants to air their dirty laundry in public. Perhaps there are solutions that they can discuss in private that they could not (or would not) discuss if the mediation were public. Further, if we want the settlement discussions between disputants to be public, we should require all negotiations to settle lawsuits to be public and require all settlements to be published.

Some people are concerned that powerful litigants can take advantage of weaker litigants and abuse the mediation process. Courts have procedural safeguards to help the weak. As I discuss in Chapter 12, 'Power Imbalances', it is true that people in dispute do not usually have the same level of power: one party is usually more powerful. It is also true that the powerful person may get a better deal at mediation. Is that inappropriate? Do we want to take away power from people who have it and give it to people who do not, just because the disputants are in litigation? Even if the answer to the question is yes, does a court really balance power? The person with the greater resources can use the litigation process to his or her advantage and benefit from the power that that person yields. Further, if we do not like the fact that people reach agreements based (at least partly) on the fact that there is a power imbalance, don't we again have to prevent settlement negotiations and require people to go to trial? Does that really help the disempowered person? Mediation, at least, introduces a neutral person who can facilitate the discussion and ensure that people have an opportunity to communicate.

Mediation can open wounds and result in disputants bringing up issues that would be irrelevant at trial. Is that bad? If the issues are festering, mediation can bring those issues to the surface and the disputants can work through them. In fact, it may be as a result of the fact that those issues have been raised that creative solutions are uncovered.

Many lawyers argue that mediation, particularly before discovery, is premature and should wait until more information is known. It is true that more information enables lawyers and disputants to make a better assessment of their cases. But limited information does not prevent them from making an assessment of the case before discovery. Business people make assessments and decisions all the time based on imperfect information. More information may make the case stronger, but it may also make it weaker.

An early mediation can result in an early settlement and can take people out of the litigation process early. Is that a good or a bad thing? To answer that question, we need to have a closer look at the litigation process and compare it to mediation.

2.2   THE LITIGATION PROCESS

Litigation is society's answer to conflict between two people that they cannot resolve themselves. They retain lawyers, go through pleadings, written and oral discovery, various motions, pre-trial procedures and a trial. At the end, the judge makes a decision that may or may not be appealed. Once the disputants initiate the process, it takes on a life of its own, and disputants often become frustrated with it.

That is not to suggest that there isn't a place for litigation; litigation is necessary to resolve conflict that cannot be resolved in some other way. Mediation operates 'in the shadow of the law';[5] it does not operate in a vacuum. Disputants in mediation know that if they do not settle their dispute, they will proceed to trial. The litigation process is not perfect, however, and there are a number of reasons why disputants may want to have an early mediation in an attempt to get out of the litigation process.

2.2.1   Cost

Lawsuits are expensive. Legal victories are sometimes hollow because the cost to both sides of trying the case can exceed the amount of the judgment. Because of the high cost, litigation is increasingly being viewed as justifiable only for large corporations and only when there is a significant amount in dispute. There are legal fees, filing fees and costs that can be awarded against the losing disputant (in jurisdictions where costs are awarded). It is not unusual for litigation to cost each disputant £50,000 and it is not unusual for it to cost each side over £100,000 in complex cases.

As previously stated, mediation is usually designed to start and finish in one day. Fees for the mediator range from zero (volunteer mediators) to about £10,000 per day for the most expensive mediators. Half-day mediations are not uncommon. The disputants usually share the cost of the mediator. The total cost of the mediation, even if there is no settlement, therefore usually pales in comparison to the cost of litigation.

In some jurisdictions, courts have punished disputants who have refused to participate in mediation by refusing to award costs to the victorious party when costs would otherwise have been awarded if the disputant refused to participate in a mediation.[6] The cost of not attempting mediation, therefore, can be severe.

Mediation reduces the costs of resolving the dispute.

---

5   This phrase is generally attributed to Professor Robert Mnookin of Harvard Law School.
6   See, eg, *Dunnett v Railtrack plc* [2002] EWCA Civ 302 (CA). Note also the Woolf reforms that encourage the use of mediation.

2.2.2   Time

The wheels of justice grind slowly. It takes a long time from the commencement of a lawsuit until judgment. While the length of the litigation process varies from jurisdiction to jurisdiction, for significant cases it is rare for a case to be heard in less than a year, and not at all uncommon for three years to elapse between the time of the commencement of the lawsuit and the judgment at trial.

Even after the trial, the process may not be over. The losing disputant may appeal and it may be a year (or even more) before a final decision is handed down on appeal. During the appeal there will, of course, be more costs to the disputants.

Over time, memories fade, and the fact that it takes a long time from the commencement of a lawsuit to judgment means that it is less likely that the truth will be determined. Also, companies that are fighting lawsuits must report on their annual reports that there is outstanding litigation, and sometimes set aside money as a contingency in case the lawsuit is lost.

Mediations can often be scheduled within a week of the request for mediation. While some mediators and some lawyers are busy and schedules may necessitate a slightly longer wait, it is unusual for disputants to have to wait more than a month or two for a mediation date.

Mediation reduces the time that it takes to resolve a dispute.

2.2.3   Time away from other things

When you are involved in litigation, you do not have as much time for activites that you would prefer to be doing. For business people, the impact of being involved in litigation should not be underestimated. The primary objective of businesspeople is to run the business effectively and to make a profit, not to fight lawsuits. Time that is taken away from the business is time that is not spent productively. For individuals, time spent involved in litigation is time spent away from family, from work and from other activities.

During the litigation process, the disputants must find all relevant documents, provide the facts to their lawyers, help their lawyers prepare for discovery and trial, prepare themselves for trial, and participate in discovery and trial. They also participate in settlement discussions if there are any.

Early settlement allows people to spend their time in more productive ways.

2.2.4   Emotional cost

Litigation is an emotional process. It is rarely fun. People who are not used to the process (and even those who are) often find it stressful. It causes sleepless nights as litigants consider what they have said, what they should have said, what they will say, how unfair the process is, what may come out under cross-examination and the consequences of losing. People may also be concerned about the consequences of having their dispute played out on a public stage and the effect that that will have on their reputations. The stress and emotional cost of litigation can translate into less focus on work and may create conflict in personal life.

One of the goals of mediation is to allow disputants to resolve their dispute while avoiding many of the stresses associated with litigation. Often the best stress reliever is early settlement of the dispute.

Mediation can reduce the stress involved in resolving conflict.

2.2.5   Public versus private

Litigation is public. The public has the right to attend court and the press can comment on the proceedings in the newspaper and on the evening news. It is not always in the litigants' best interest to have their issues resolved in public. The issues in dispute may be confidential ones that a disputant does not want to share with others. Litigants may be embarrassed about the allegations made against them and may not want those allegations to be made public, regardless of whether or not they are true.

In mediation, the process is almost always confidential, unless the disputants decide to make it public. Since the process and the resolution are confidential, those not involved in the dispute need never find out the confessions that were made or the settlement that was reached.

Mediation is a confidential process.

2.2.6   Creative solutions

A judge has jurisdiction to make specific decisions based on the evidence presented in court. If the judge makes a decision outside the court's jurisdiction, the decision will be overturned on appeal.

Judges have jurisdiction to provide for certain remedies and cannot order other remedies, even when they believe that other remedies are appropriate. Judges are only empowered to decide the issues before them, even if the solution to those issues is best tied to other issues. Judges are not allowed to look for creative solutions. They are not permitted to expand the list of possible options to see if the particular case would be best served by a solution that was not argued and that the application of the law would not allow.

For example, if a homeowner is having a dispute with her neighbour about the fact that the neighbour is unfriendly, has a fence encroaching on her yard by six inches, and has a dog that barks 24 hours a day, the homeowner may take the dispute to a lawyer, and would tell the lawyer about the 'problem'. The lawyer would take the problem and turn it into a 'case'. The lawyer may attempt to obtain an order to have the dog muzzled during hours when the city by-laws prohibit excessive noise, and an order that the fence be moved the six inches. These are possible orders the judge could make. The judge cannot order the neighbours to be nice to each other, or have the neighbours work together to find mutually convenient times for the dog to visit a relative. Even if the homeowner with the problem wins the case, the neighbour may be madder and ruder than ever, and the dog may now howl because he is muzzled in the evening. The case may be won but the problem may not be solved.

Mediation, on the other hand, is designed to allow for the exploration of creative options, and to allow disputants to explore all of the possible solutions to a problem. The discussion in the mediation is not restricted to the legal issues in dispute; the discussion can encompass ideas for creative solutions, and possible solutions to problems that are not the subject of the litigation. The solutions could involve an apology, an agreement to act in a particular way, a future joint venture or another creative solution that a court could not impose.

It Happened at Mediation

I once mediated a dispute between a marina owner and a township about whether the marina owner should be required to spend a significant amount of money to clean up his marina to meet town guidelines. He restored old boats and had a number of boats on the shore that were partially restored. The town had received complaints about the mess on his land that could be seen by the boats that went past the marina. The marina owner believed that he should be able to do what he liked on his land. He believed that people on the town council disliked him and that the town guidelines were drafted to deal specifically with him. The township believed that the marina owner refused to clean up his land for the express purpose of breaching township guidelines because of his personal antagonism toward the town.

At the commencement of the mediation, the marina owner vented his anger at the town council representative and expressed in no uncertain terms that there was nothing that could be agreed that would cause him to clean up his land. The town would have to remove him kicking and screaming. The town representative said that he was prepared to do whatever was necessary to force the marina owner to abide by the town's guidelines.

After a time, tempers calmed down and the marina owner explained his difficult financial position and described the stress that was created by the town's attempts to enforce guidelines that he believed were not being broken. The town representative that had contacted him (who was not present at the mediation) had been rude and always demanded that the owner clean up his 'mess' within a couple of hours. The marina owner explained that if he gave in to every request that the town representative made, he would not be able to earn a living. The town representative at the mediation explained that the town had a duty to investigate complaints and make sure that everyone in the town abided by all of the guidelines.

Through discussion at the mediation, each of the disputants learned of the other's perspective. Each side began to understand the constraints of the other, and each side eventually apologised to the other for what they had done. Once a level of trust had been re-established, the two sides were able to come to an arrangement that worked for both of them. The marina owner agreed to keep two of the boats (that were the subject of the majority of the complaints) in a garage, and the town agreed that the owner would be given at least a week to clean up any 'mess' that contravened town guidelines. The town representative also agreed to have someone other than the person who had been rude call the owner in the event of a complaint.

Mediation allows for creative solutions.

2.2.7 People can express themselves

People need to say what is on their minds and why they are upset. In litigation that opportunity does not always exist. Litigants can answer questions when the rules allow them to answer, either before or at trial. In answering questions, the disputants are limited to speaking about issues that are relevant to the litigation. There is no opportunity for them to talk about how the litigation has affected them, to complain about the other person's non-responsiveness or to vent their emotions about what has occurred.

The mediation process provides an opportunity for disputants to express in their own words the issues of importance to them, uninterrupted. People are not limited to the issues in dispute and can say whatever they want directly to others involved in the dispute. Disputants sometimes have a need to get issues off their chests and may not be open to explore solutions until they have had the opportunity to express their emotions. Sometimes they express themselves to the other side and at other times they are more comfortable expressing themselves to the mediator in a private meeting (caucus).

When complaints, emotions and personal attacks are expressed directly to the other disputant, it is the role of the mediator to take the comments and reframe them to facilitate rather than destroy opportunities for settlement. When the comments are expressed in caucus, the mediator will listen to the attacks and try to understand the perspective of the person making the attacks.

It Happened at Mediation

At some mediations, people come in with entrenched positions and threats about what they will do if the other side does not agree to their position. I was mediating a case in which a courier for an insurance company had been employed for 30 years, was 70 years old and was asked to retire. He was furious that, after he had given so much of his life to the company, it would ask him to leave. He was so hurt that he had decided, before the mediation, that he was going to go to the press and mount a public relations campaign that he believed would cripple the insurance company. He wanted the company to pay for how it had treated him.

He did not want to talk directly to the insurance company representative, his former supervisor, and requested that the entire mediation take place with the disputants in separate rooms. I acceded to his request, as the other side did not mind having the mediation conducted entirely in caucus.

For the first four hours of the mediation, he told me how upset he was at the way the company had treated him and what he planned to do during his public relations campaign. I was careful not to argue with him, not to talk about whether his campaign would work, and not to talk about the benefits to him of settling his case. I spent the entire four hours listening and showing him that I understood what he was saying and believed that he would mount his campaign.

At the end of the four hours, he was both tired and relieved. He felt that I understood him and was comfortable that I believed that he would act. He knew that I was taking him seriously and not dismissing him out of hand. We then discussed the effort that he would have to undertake in his campaign, the cost of the effort, the time it would take, and the stress on him (as he had recently suffered a stroke). He decided that if he could negotiate a good settlement, that would make more sense to him than undertaking his campaign. He could only move toward settlement, however, after he had had the opportunity to tell me his story and be taken seriously.

> The two sides then presented settlement offers and counter-offers, and eventually settled on the basis that the company make a payment to the courier of an amount that both sides believed was fair. The courier then decided that it was time for him to go into the room where the insurance company representatives were caucusing to shake hands with his supervisor. With the animosity gone, the courier and his former supervisor embraced.

It is not uncommon, even at the end of a mediation where the dispute did not settle, for the disputants to report that they thought the process was a good one. This can be due, in large part, to the fact that they had the opportunity to express what was on their minds.

Mediation provides an opportunity to express emotions and views.

2.2.8   Unpredictability

Despite the best efforts of all involved, litigation can be unpredictable. There are a number of reasons why. First, no matter how well witnesses are prepared, they may say unexpected things on the witness stand. They may get nervous, they may be overwhelmed by the process or may remember things on the stand that they had previously forgotten. Secondly, surprises sometimes occur at trial, no matter how well prepared a disputant is. Thirdly, cross-examination may reveal flaws in witnesses' testimony.

Both sides will argue the law and argue the cases that they believe apply to the facts so as to support their positions. In the end, the judge will decide on the law that applies. If the issue were completely predictable, there would be no need to go to court. It is specifically because the issue is somewhat unpredictable that it is necessary for a judge to make a decision.

Lawyers, through their experience, predict the likely outcome at trial. Unfortunately, lawyers on opposite sides of a dispute rarely (if ever) agree on the likely outcome at trial. Each side usually believes that its analysis of the case is better than the other side's, though both sides usually recognise that no case is 100% predictable. As a result, there is a risk in going to trial and putting the decision in the hands of the judge.

There is no guarantee that a judge will find the truth. Judges are human and humans make mistakes. It would be naïve to believe that judges can always accurately assess who is lying and who is telling the truth in court.

There is no decision-maker in mediation. Even in an evaluative mediation, the mediator gives an opinion but leaves the decision in the hands of the disputants. The process belongs to the disputants and only they decide on the result and whether the case settles.

Mediation will not impose an unpredictable result on disputants.

2.2.9   Expertise of decision-maker

Judges are former lawyers and many are former barristers. They are appointed after having distinguished careers in law. Some of them practised commercial litigation, some criminal law, some administrative law and others family law. Most judges work very hard to learn the law relevant to the cases before them and do their best to make informed and reasoned decisions. There is no guarantee, however, that the judge will be an expert in the area in dispute.

In mediation, you can select a mediator with substantive or technical expertise. The disputants can choose whom they want to mediate their cases and they will often opt for a mediator with experience in the area of dispute. Further, as the mediator is not the decision-maker, it is not so important for the mediator to have complete substantive expertise. It is necessary for the mediator to understand the issues well enough to be able to communicate effectively with the disputants, but it is the disputants, not the mediator, who resolve the dispute and decide on the solution.

Disputants can choose mediators who are expert in the area of the dispute.

2.2.10 Win/lose

In litigation, there is a winner and a loser. In some cases, there are two losers, as both sides believe that the judge did not decide the case correctly. In mediation, there will only be an agreement if both (or all) disputants agree, and therefore there will only be an agreement if there are two winners, or two disputants who believe that the result in mediation is more of a win for both of them than proceeding to litigation.

Mediation can produce win/win solutions.

2.2.11 Relationship destroyed

It is rare for litigation to conclude by having the disputants walk over to each other, shake hands and say, 'that was fun; let's do it again sometime'. Usually, at the end of litigation, the disputants hate each other and the relationship is irreparably damaged. Rarely will the disputants be able to mend their relationship to the point where they can maintain business or personal relationships. After litigation, people usually conclude that it is not worth the risk to maintain a relationship with a former adversary.

In mediation, the structure is not an adversarial one and the disputants need not consider themselves adversaries. The process allows both sides to talk about what has gone wrong, to leave the past in the past and to see if there are opportunities to work together in the future. They focus on how they can solve a problem rather than on how they can defeat each other.

As stated earlier, the number one rule of mediation is, above all, do no harm; that is, make sure that the disputants do not leave the mediation in a worse position than when they arrived. This includes the state of their relationship. Through the discussion and the exploration of options, mediations often result in creative solutions that have the former adversaries working together in a new venture. Not all mediations end with repaired relationships; however, most mediations end with the disputants believing that their relationship is no worse than when the mediation commenced.

It Happened at Mediation

Two men had been in business together for 11 years and each owned shares in a closely held company. They had a dispute because one of the men perceived that he was working significantly harder than the other and should be compensated accordingly. The other disagreed.

When the mediation commenced, I was told by the lawyers for each shareholder that the two men hated each other, did not want to be in the same room together, and were unlikely to agree on anything.

The entire mediation was conducted with the two men in different rooms. At the end of the mediation, the disputants reached an agreement where one would purchase the shares of the other at an agreed price. Once the deal was finalised, the two men got together, shook hands and started talking. It turned out that the one who perceived that he was a harder worker (the purchaser) thought that the other person was a valuable contributor to the company, and maybe not such a bad person after all. The purchaser offered the seller a job at the company, and the seller accepted.

Once the dispute had been resolved, two 'enemies' became friends again and found that they could do more together than they could do alone.

Mediation preserves and sometimes enhances relationships.

2.2.12 Control over the process

In litigation, the process is determined by the rules of court, and by the judge; the disputants have no control over it. They are told where to sit, when to stand, when to speak and even when to bow. They have no control over who presents issues first, whether they are allowed to drink coffee while they are in court or when the process will finish that day.

All of these process issues are in the control of the disputants in mediation. While the mediator is generally considered to be responsible for managing the process, the disputants can dictate what the mediator does, not vice versa. The mediator must adapt to the process suggested by the disputants and the process need not be a formal one.

The process in mediation is in the hands of the disputants.

2.2.13 A fair and appropriate result

Litigation is designed to produce a fair and appropriate result. Judges apply law that has been developed over many years to create justice and fairness. Unfortunately, the law does not always produce justice. Common law developed from cases with specific facts, and those facts may not be applicable to the current facts; nevertheless, the law will be applied (and if it is not, the decision will be overturned on appeal).

Mediation also strives to achieve justice and fairness. The difference is that the disputants, not the courts, set the standard of justice and fairness or reasonableness (for facilitative mediations).

Disputants need only enter into an agreement if they believe it is fair and just to do so. If they fail to reach an agreement, they can still take their issue to court and have the court apply its standard of justice.

In mediation, the disputants, not the courts, set the standard of fairness.

2.2.14 Process for future disputes

The court process is not an easily accessible one. People do not have access to a judge every time they have a dispute, no matter how small. It is a process of last resort.

In mediation, the disputants not only resolve their conflict, they go through a process that they can use to solve disputes that may arise in the future, either with respect to the implementation of the agreement or in another context. If future disputes arise, the disputants will have a better understanding of how they can communicate in a way that will allow them to resolve their new conflict amicably. This is true not just for transformative mediations, but also for facilitative ones.

Mediation teaches a process that helps people resolve future conflict.

2.2.15 Decisions are not imposed

When decisions are imposed on people, by a court, by a superior or by anyone else, people may resist the decisions (even when the decisions are good ones) since they did not come up with or have ownership in the decisions. People rarely like to have decisions imposed on them. As they are forced to implement the decision, they may resist and attempt to undermine a decision that they believe is unfair.

In mediation, the disputants have ownership in the decision and the issue is resolved only if both (or all) of the disputants agree. If the disputants have ownership in the decision, they are more likely to implement it.

Mediation leaves decision-making in the hands of the disputants, making successful implementation of the agreement more likely.

2.2.16 Learn more

For lawyers who do not believe in the appropriateness of mediation, who believe it is only an obstacle to getting to court, there is a purely pragmatic reason to mediate and it has nothing to do with settlement. Through the mediation process, a disputant may acquire information about the other disputant's case, his or her perspective on the case and about the strengths and weaknesses of their own case. Even if the case does not settle, the disputants may get information through the mediation process that will help them at trial. While the process is without prejudice (discussed later in Chapter 5, 'Setting the Table'), and while there is no requirement to disclose information in mediation, disputants and lawyers may learn information that they can prove through further investigation and that information may help them obtain a favourable settlement, or a better result at trial.

While some mediators are uncomfortable with this pragmatic view of mediation, others accept it and even think of it as a tool that they can use to help facilitate communication between disputants.

It Happened at Mediation

I was a mediator for a personal injury dispute between an insurance company and a claimant. The claimant had severely injured his legs in a car accident and was suing the insurance company for unpaid benefits. The insurance company representative arrived at the mediation (with his lawyer) early and we were chatting while we waited for the claimant (and lawyer) to arrive. I try to avoid discussing the case during this preliminary stage and we were talking of matters not related to the mediation. Out of the blue, the insurance representative said: 'By the way, I have no intention of settling at this mediation. I'm here for two purposes. The first is to find out as much information as possible about the claimant that will help me at trial. The second is to speak directly to the claimant about the strength of our case because I am not convinced that the claimant is getting the whole story from his lawyer. I just thought I should tell you, in confidence of course, that I have no intention of settling this case today.'

My first reaction was that I should resign as mediator because I was facilitating a process where I knew that one disputant was not acting in what I then believed was good faith. I believed that, unless both sides were prepared to make a genuine attempt to settle the dispute, they were not acting in good faith. On further reflection, however, I decided that the insurance representative was not acting in bad faith after all. He had told me that he was there to communicate. He wanted to listen and he wanted to speak. There was no particular bad faith. Was there any more that I could ask of a participant at a mediation than a willingness to listen and a willingness to speak? If the insurance representative did not want to settle, that was his prerogative, and he was perfectly entitled to go to court. I decided to conduct the mediation.

The session was initially acrimonious, with the insurance company lawyer presenting strong arguments as to why the company should not have to pay a lot of money for an injury that it believed was not serious. The insurance company representative talked about the claimant's demands and suggested that they were not reasonable when the injuries to his legs were compared to court awards for those who sustained extremely serious injuries to their entire bodies. The representative presented examples of awards that were made to others who had injured their legs. The company believed that the claimant could return to work any time he wanted (he was then off work) because his injuries were to his legs and he had a sedentary job.

The claimant talked about his leg pain and about the difficulties he had sitting. He talked about his job and the tasks he was required to perform.

The insurance company learned more about the claimant's job and decided that, while the company representative still believed that the claimant could return to work, there was a risk that a court could find that it would be too difficult for him to return. The claimant learned that, despite the fact that he wanted a lot of money, the court awards for his type of injury were much lower than the amounts he was demanding.

After six hours, the case settled when the insurance company offered to pay an amount that the claimant found acceptable.

Mediation provides an opportunity to gather information.

2.3   WHEN IS MEDIATION NOT APPROPRIATE?

I do not want to suggest that, because there are so many reasons to mediate, mediation is always appropriate. There are situations where I believe mediation is not appropriate. Basically, mediation is not appropriate if negotiation is not appropriate, and if settlement (of any kind) is not appropriate. If it makes sense to try to work things out, it usually makes sense to mediate. Sometimes, though, it does not make sense to settle and therefore does not make sense to mediate.

A decision to attend a mediation is not a decision to settle. It is a decision to explore the possibility of settlement and to see if there is a settlement that makes more sense for both disputants than continuing with the dispute. If there is not, the case should not settle.

2.3.1 Precedent

In some cases, the precedent is more important to at least one of the disputants than is the substantive outcome. For example, if a company has numerous pieces of outstanding litigation and needs a precedent in one piece in order to deal with the others, the company may take the strongest of the cases to trial in order to get a precedent to help it deal with the other cases. In such a situation, settlement may not be appropriate so mediation may not be appropriate.

It Happened at Mediation

I was mediating a dispute in a mandatory mediation (a mediation ordered by the court) where the claimant had been injured as a result of a fall on a pavement. There had been construction work on the pavement and there had been no warning that it may be hazardous to walk on the pavement. The claimant sued the city for not keeping the pavement in good repair and the city cross-claimed against the construction company that it had hired to work on the pavement.

It turned out that the construction company had a number of lawsuits with the city, all relating to the construction company's alleged negligence in repairing pavement throughout the last three years. It emerged that the agreement between the city and the construction company stated that the company would inform the city when it was finished with the construction, and the city would then have the responsibility of cleaning the pavement so that it was not a danger.

In all of the lawsuits the city was arguing that the company should not have left the pavement in an unsafe condition until the city had completed its clean-up.

In the case that I was mediating, the evidence was that the construction work on the pavement had finished three years before the injury had occurred. The construction company had told the city that the construction work was finished and the city had not yet cleaned up the pavement.

At the mediation, the construction company told me that the facts of this case were favourable to the construction company compared to the facts of the other cases. Because the company had completed the work three years prior, the company was confident that it would not be held liable for the fact that the city had not yet cleaned the pavement of debris. All of the other cases related to work that was completed within the past year. The company decided, therefore, that it was not in its interest to participate in a settlement. It preferred to have the matter go to trial and have a precedent set that it could use to negotiate favourable results with the city in its other cases.

> The claimant was set on receiving at least $35,000 in damages and the city was only offering $25,000, trying to persuade the construction company to pay the last $10,000. The construction company refused to contribute anything to the settlement.
>
> In the end, the city agreed to pay the extra $10,000 because it feared that, if the case went to court, it may not like the precedent that would be set.

2.3.2   Constitutional and other legal issues

Sometimes constitutional or other strictly legal issues need to be resolved by a court and not by settlement. In such situations, mediation may be inappropriate. One must be careful, however, not to eliminate mediation as an option for cases that have legal issues. A lot of these cases do settle and are appropriate for mediation. Often, the constitutional or other legal issue is only one of many issues, and solutions can be achieved that are better for both disputants than proceeding to trial. If there are individuals or companies that could benefit from an early settlement, then mediation could be appropriate.

2.3.3   Everyone has a reason to go to trial

There are some situations in which all of the disputants have valid reasons for wanting a trial, and a settlement would not work for anyone, regardless of the terms of the settlement. It may be that the cost of litigation and other incentives to settle do not apply in a particular case and trial therefore makes sense for both sides.

It Happened at Mediation

I was a mediator at a mandatory mediation where a car leasing company was suing a person who had returned a car in the middle of a lease and was refusing to pay the balance owing on the lease. The individual said that someone at the car company had told him that he could return the car and no further payments would be owing. The leasing company denied that it had given the individual permission to return the car with no fee owing. The amount in dispute seemed to be about £1,500 and I was convinced (when I read the material prior to the mediation) that there would be a quick settlement once everyone realised that litigation would not make a lot of sense for either side. I soon learned an important lesson.

I found out in the mediation that the leasing company was using a new in-house lawyer who did not have a lot of litigation experience. The company was happy for the lawyer to gain court experience and the cost would be minimal as the lawyer was on salary. Further, there were a number of the leasing company's customers who were watching to see whether the leasing company settled or proceeded to trial (because they also wanted to return cars early). The leasing company wanted to show that it would fight to recover the money it believed was owing if people returned cars early. Regardless of the outcome at trial, the leasing company believed that taking the matter to court would be a deterrent to others who were considering returning a car early.

The person who returned the car early, the defendant, had retired two years earlier. He was a doctor but had spent the last 25 years being an expert witness in litigation. He believed that he could do a better job litigating than the lawyers he had watched for so many years. He was representing himself in the case and was not going to be denied his opportunity to prove that he could be as good a barrister as any lawyer.

Although there was a small amount in dispute, the disputants had a vested interest in not settling and in going to trial. No deal was, in this case, the preferred result for them.

2.3.4   The disputants can settle on their own

There is no point spending time and money on mediation if the disputants and their lawyers can settle the case easily without the help of a mediator. While this may sound obvious, there are situations where people get caught up in the benefits of mediation and forget that people may be able to work things out for themselves. Mediation should only be attempted after people have talked and determined that they cannot settle the dispute on their own.

It Happened At Mediation

I was the mediator for a breach of contract dispute. When one of the disputants talked about her perspective on the dispute and what she was looking for in terms of a settlement, the other disputant asked for a private caucus with me. The lawyer told me that he was baffled, since what the other side was asking for was what they had been prepared to settle for all along. He asked if we needed to continue with the process or whether they could just begin drafting a settlement document. We drafted a settlement document and the case was resolved in less than an hour. If the lawyers had communicated before the mediation and attempted to settle, they would have discovered that mediation was not necessary.

2.3.5   Potential for violence, abuse or similar unacceptable conduct

As you will recall, the first rule of mediation is, above all, do no harm. There are some situations where one of the disputants is physically afraid of the other – sometimes for good reason. The mediation process should not increase the likelihood that physical violence will occur. Some mediators are trained in techniques to use when there is a threat of violence (such as, for example, conducting the entire mediation with the disputants in separate rooms). Even well-trained mediators may not be able to prevent violence from occurring in some situations, however. Where there is a threat of violence, it should be the rare situation where mediation is undertaken.

Tips for Lawyers

- It is true that, if mediation results in the settlement of a case, your fees for that case will be lower than they would otherwise have been. If that is a concern for you, you must ask yourself whether the decision about whether to mediate should be based on your interests or on the client's interest. If mediation makes sense for the client, you have a duty to recommend it.

- Further, if you earn a reputation as someone who settles cases, who gets good deals for your clients, who is an effective advocate at mediation, you may find a significant increase in the size of your practice (as has been the experience of a number of lawyers who have embraced mediation).

- When deciding whether it makes sense for you and your client to propose mediation or consent to participate in a mediation proposed by the other side, you may want to consider the possible costs that a judge may impose on a disputant who refuses to participate in a mediation.

- If you do mediate and the case does not settle, you can assure your client that you have made the attempt to settle, and it will be the client's decision to reject the other side's proposal and carry on with the litigation. The client may be less concerned about the cost of litigation knowing that you have made every effort to settle and avoid the extra cost.

- If you settle the cases that can settle at mediation, that will leave you more time to focus on the cases that do not settle and require the extra effort to prepare for trial.

- Where there is a precedent that must be established, where there is a constitutional or other legal issue that must be decided, or where everyone has a good reason to go to trial, mediation may not be appropriate. A good test is to ask yourself how you would react if the other lawyer called you asking to talk about settlement. If your reaction would be to listen, mediation could be helpful; if your reaction would be to say that you do not want to settle under any circumstances, you should not proceed to mediation.

- Even where you believe that mediation is not appropriate and is not likely to result in settlement, it may be in your (and in your client's) interest to attend a mediation because you may learn something that helps you if the matter does go to trial. Most people are open to talk and listen in mediation and you may obtain valuable information and improve your client's case for trial.

- Your client may want to attempt mediation to: reduce cost; end the dispute quickly; spend time on enjoyable activities rather than on litigation; reduce stress; resolve conflict in private; explore possible creative solutions; avoid an imposed and unpredictable result; and find a solution that preserves a relationship.

- As for the timing of the mediation, you may believe that, if you mediate later rather than sooner, you will have more information and will be in a better position to get a better deal for your client. That may be true, though it also may be true that you will be in a worse position and may get a worse deal. All that you know for sure is that your client will have to spend more money to get there, and if the client is unhappy about that, your reputation could be affected.

- If there is a potential for violence in the dispute, determine whether the mediator you have selected is experienced in dealing with potentially violent situations. Do not engage in mediation without safeguards for your client (such as a guarantee that the disputants will never be in the same room).

Tips for Mediators

- Mediation can: reduce the cost of resolving the dispute; resolve the dispute quickly; allow disputants to focus on more enjoyable activities; reduce the stress associated with conflict; resolve conflict privately; result in creative solutions; allow people to express their views directly to the other side; avoid unpredictable results from being imposed; result in a win/win outcome; avoid further destruction of relationships; allow disputants to determine what is fair; and allow disputants to obtain information that can help them if the case does not settle.

- Even with all of these advantages of mediation, some people may not be persuaded to go down that route. For those people, you will need to find out why they do not want to go to mediation, talk about their concerns, and see how those concerns might be met. You will need to be open to the idea that it may not be best for them to go to mediation.

- If you suspect that one of the disputants is in physical danger, separate them immediately and discuss the issue with them to see if your suspicion is valid. If it appears to you that there is a potential for violence, you may choose to end the mediation or contact someone who is expert in conducting mediation with potentially violent people.

CHAPTER 3

MEDIATION: FACILITATED NEGOTIATION

What is mediation? What magic does it bring to disputants to help them solve a problem that they could not solve themselves? How does it work?

Mediation is nothing more and nothing less than facilitated negotiation. The best mediators are experts in the process of negotiation and help disputants overcome obstacles in negotiation. To be an effective advocate in a mediation, a lawyer must be an effective negotiator; to be an effective conflict resolver, a mediator must be an expert negotiator and problem solver.

Most negotiators can be placed in one of three categories: competitive bargainers; co-operative bargainers; and principled bargainers.

3.1 THE COMPETITIVE BARGAINER

3.1.1 What does the competitive bargainer do?

Competitive bargaining is a common style of negotiating. The competitive or positional bargainer is focused on the outcome of the negotiation, becomes entrenched in positions and does not like to make concessions. When competitive bargainers make concessions, they do so grudgingly. Competitive bargainers use techniques that encourage other negotiators to make concessions, so that these other negotiators will move as close as possible to their bottom lines.

The competitive bargainer focuses on the psychology of the other negotiator, trying to out-think the other person in the negotiation, trying to get the other person to make concessions so that the competitive bargainer will reach the best results.

The stereotypical competitive bargainer will sometimes do whatever is necessary to achieve a good substantive deal. Some competitive bargainers will bluff, accuse, cheat, intimidate, create false issues, lie or use whatever techniques are necessary to get a good deal.

Obviously, there are competitive bargainers who do not fall into the stereotype. These negotiators, while extremely concerned with substantive results, believe that they are doing what is just in the circumstances. They do not consider themselves competitive; they usually define themselves as 'tough but fair'. They believe that they are skilled at seeing the 'fair' outcome, and they will do what they can to move everyone to that outcome. They often believe that others in negotiation are unreasonable and cannot see the obvious and fair solution that is being put forward.

Other competitive bargainers are passive/aggressive. They create a facade of being co-operative, trying to get the other side's confidence, while all the time strategising how they can take advantage of others in the negotiation.

3.1.2 Advantages

There are certainly advantages to competitive bargaining for the competitive bargainer. First and most importantly, the competitive bargainer often gets good substantive results. By taking a more aggressive approach in negotiation, the competitive bargainer often forces others to make concessions and agree to do things that they would not otherwise have done.

A second advantage is that colleagues, clients and constituents often respect them. The competitive bargainer develops a reputation for being tough and for getting results, and therefore others like to hire him or her to negotiate for them.

The fact that the competitive bargainer has a reputation for being tough may also assist him or her in getting a good deal in the negotiation, as the others may make concessions based on the competitive bargainer's reputation.

Another advantage of competitive bargaining is that it helps the negotiator maintain focus. Competitive bargainers know what it is they want to achieve and are rarely distracted by peripheral issues. Competitive negotiators keep the negotiation focused on reaching a resolution of the issues being negotiated.

Because competitive negotiators keep things focused, they can sometimes complete negotiations faster than other negotiators. They do not waste time on small talk or peripheral issues, preferring to focus on the issues that need to be resolved.

They also do not let conflict fester so that it reaches unnecessarily high levels. Because they address conflict head on and are not afraid of it, issues can be dealt with before they become larger issues.

3.1.3   Disadvantages

Why not be a competitive bargainer then? Isn't negotiation all about getting the best results? Perhaps not.

Maybe the most significant disadvantage of competitive bargaining is that, if the other negotiator is also competitive, an unnecessary deadlock can result. The disputants may not reach a deal even where there are many possible good deals that could be reached – a large zone of possible agreement. Their obstinance, persistence and focus on trying to get the 'best' deal and to get the other side to make further concessions may prevent them from coming to an agreement at all.

A further disadvantage to being competitive is that the relationship between disputants may be irreparably destroyed through the negotiation process. A damaged relationship can be problematic in two contexts. First, any agreement must be implemented. If the relationship is damaged, the disputants may have difficulty implementing the deal that is reached as each side attempts to gain an advantage over the other in the implementation. Secondly, there may be future negotiations. Rarely is a negotiation a one-time-only situation. The world is a global village and people run into each other again and again, even when they live in different countries. If the competitive negotiator damages the relationship, the other side may try to exact revenge in future negotiations when the power dynamics are reversed.

As for the competitive bargainer's reputation, even though clients and constituents may appreciate and respect it, other negotiators may not. In the future, when other negotiators have a choice of negotiation partners, they may choose not to deal with the competitive bargainer with whom they have had a bad experience.

In addition, competitive negotiators may miss opportunities to find creative solutions that could solve difficult problems. Because competitive negotiators are so focused on getting the best deal (as they perceive it going into the negotiation), they may not search for the creative or 'pie-expanding' answers to difficult problems.

Finally, competitive bargaining may prolong negotiations. While competitive negotiators do focus on the issues, they also spend time posturing and arguing – time that could be more valuably spent problem-solving.

3.2   CO-OPERATIVE BARGAINING

3.2.1   What does the co-operative bargainer do?

At the other end of the spectrum is the co-operative bargainer. This is the person who is keenly aware of the disadvantages of competitive bargaining and is extremely concerned about the relationship in a negotiation. The co-operative bargainer will do whatever is necessary to reach an agreement and preserve the relationship, even if that involves making substantive concessions. The co-operative bargainer judges the success of a negotiation by two criteria: whether an agreement has been reached; and whether both sides are happy with the agreement and the process. Co-operative bargainers are concerned about future negotiations and how other negotiators view them.

3.2.2   Advantages

There are a number of advantages in taking a co-operative approach to negotiating. One advantage is that the co-operative bargainer usually has a good relationship with the other disputant at the end of the negotiation. As a result, it may be easier to implement the agreement that has been reached and future negotiations may be smoother.

Co-operative negotiators look for creative options to overcome obstacles and try to use creative solutions to get past seemingly unsolvable problems. If there is a deal to be found, the co-operative bargainer will find it.

People often look for cues from the other negotiator to determine how to negotiate. The co-operative bargainer, by being open to make concessions, often causes the other negotiator to make concessions because the other negotiator feels comfortable with the co-operative bargainer and reflects his or her behaviour.

People like to negotiate with co-operative bargainers. As a result, when people have a choice of negotiation partners, they are often anxious to choose co-operative bargainers. The co-operative bargainer may therefore have opportunities that the competitive bargainer will never have.

3.2.3   Disadvantages

What could be wrong with striving to achieve a deal and making sure that both sides are happy? Unfortunately, there are disadvantages.

The most important is that the co-operative bargainer may not get a good deal. By making substantive concessions for the sake of the relationship, the co-operative bargainer may be sacrificing good results for a good relationship. Especially where the negotiator is acting on behalf of clients or constituents, it may be inappropriate to make concessions for the sake of the relationship.

Another disadvantage of co-operative bargaining is that the co-operative bargainer may develop a reputation as someone who is soft and, as a result, clients and constituents will be unlikely to want the co-operative bargainer to negotiate for them.

Finally, co-operative bargainers may not always improve the relationship between disputants. It may be that co-operative bargainers do not have the respect of the other negotiators and therefore cannot build the foundation for a solid relationship.

3.3   PRINCIPLED NEGOTIATION

So competitive and co-operative bargaining have advantages and disadvantages. What can we do then? Do we have to choose one style or the other and just live with the disadvantages? Should we choose when to use one style and when to use the other? Should we try to combine them in some way? Perhaps the best approach is one that takes advantage of the merits of both competitive and co-operative bargaining, and protects us from the disadvantages of both. That is principled negotiation.

Principled negotiation was introduced in the now famous book, *Getting to Yes*,[1] by Roger Fisher, William Ury and Bruce Patton. It provided a framework for principled negotiation that maximised the likelihood that negotiators would reach a good deal and maintain relationships. It also created a structure that a mediator could use to shift a competitive or co-operative negotiation into one that was more likely to result in a durable settlement.

Principled negotiation is now commonly described using Roger Fisher's seven elements (alternatives, interests, options, legitimacy, communication, relationship, commitment).[2] As an effective approach to negotiating, these seven elements underlie the mediation process and maximise the likelihood of settlement. They can be used by the lawyer to advocate effectively in mediation, and by the mediator to structure the mediation.

3.3.1   Alternatives

The first of the seven elements is alternatives. Alternatives are the paths that people can pursue if they do not reach an agreement in a negotiation. Principled negotiation recommends that, before the negotiation commences, negotiators think about what they might do if they are not successful in reaching an agreement with the other side.

---

1   Fisher, R, Ury, W and Patton, B, *Getting to Yes: Negotiating Agreement Without Giving In*, 2nd edn, 1991, New York: Penguin Books.

2   Fisher, R and Ertel, D, *Getting Ready to Negotiate: The Getting to Yes Workbook*, 1995, New York: Penguin Books; Fisher, R, Kopelman, E and Schneider, AK, *Beyond Machiavelli: Tools for Coping with Conflict*, 1995, New York: Penguin Books.

These possible courses of action (which they could undertake without the other side's consent) are their alternatives.

A few years ago, when my wife and I were buying a house, we found the house that we wanted and were preparing to negotiate with the vendor. The first stage of our preparation was determining our alternatives, the courses of action that we could take if we did not reach a deal with this vendor. Say, for example, the vendor decided to sell the house to someone else. What could we do that did not involve this vendor? Our alternatives included staying where we currently lived, buying a different house, renting a house or moving in with my parents.

Once we figured out our alternatives, we needed to consider which of them we would select if we had to choose from among the alternatives. If we did not buy the house that we wanted, we could not rent, stay where we were *and* buy another house, all at the same time. We had to choose, based on the information we had, which alternative made the most sense for us.

This path is known as the Best Alternative to a Negotiated Agreement (BATNA).[3] The BATNA is the course of action that a negotiator would take if that negotiator learned that no agreement could be reached with the other negotiator. The BATNA is not a number or a bottom line: it is a course of action. It could be one step or a series of steps.

Going back to the house example, we had sold the house we were living in (so we could not stay where we were), there were no houses for rent in the area we wanted to live in and we preferred not to move in with my parents. We decided that our best alternative, assuming (for preparation purposes) that we were unable to purchase the house we were looking at, would be to buy a different house.

Once a negotiator has figured out his or her BATNA, the negotiator must do two things with the BATNA: make it as concrete as possible; and make it as good as possible.

BATNAs are often not concrete. Because a BATNA is a course of action, the consequence of pursuing the BATNA may be uncertain. The negotiator can explore the possible consequences of pursuing the BATNA and, to the degree that there is uncertainty, attempt to reduce the uncertainty. In litigation, for example, where the BATNA may be going to trial (though it may be discontinuing the litigation), making the BATNA concrete could include investigating the time it will take to get to trial, the cost and the likelihood of a successful outcome at trial. That may require further legal research or factual investigation.

As for the house that we wanted to buy, once we had determined that our BATNA was to buy a different house, we had to make the BATNA concrete by figuring out which other house we would want to buy. It was not enough simply to decide that we would buy a different house. We looked at the other houses that were for sale and decided that we would try to purchase a house that was around the corner from the house that was our first choice. This house (our second choice) did not have as large a garden as our first choice, but the house was nice and the street

---

3   Fisher, Ury and Patton first used this acronym in *Getting to Yes, op cit*, fn 1.

was nice. Buying it was the best alternative to buying the house that was our first choice.

Once the negotiator has made his or her BATNA as concrete as possible, the negotiator may want to try to improve the BATNA and make it as good as possible. The better the BATNA, the more power the negotiator will have in the negotiation. The BATNA will be used in the negotiation (or mediation) as a measuring stick, to compare to any offer that is made. An agreement must be better than your best alternative, or you should not accept it. The better your BATNA, the better the negotiated agreement must be for you to accept it.

Going back to our house, once we had decided that our BATNA was buying the house with the smaller garden, we attempted to improve our BATNA. We met the agent who was selling the house with the smaller garden and discovered the asking price (which, for the sake of this example, was £300,000). After some discussion, we also learned that the vendors wanted to sell the house quickly and would be prepared to accept £25,000 less than the asking price if the sale could be completed within a month. We had the ability to do a quick completion. Our BATNA was now as concrete and as good as we could make it.

That is not to suggest that we would not have paid more than £275,000 for the house that was our first choice; we would have preferred to pay up to £330,000 for the house that was our first choice rather than buy the house with the smaller garden for £275,000. At that point we knew clearly what we would do if we did not reach an agreement to purchase the first house and any deal that we would reach on that house had to be better than buying the other house (our second choice) for £275,000.

After the negotiator has figured out the BATNA and made it as good and as concrete as it can possibly be, the negotiator should then put away the BATNA and not use it in the negotiation. The negotiator should use the other six elements (presented later in this chapter) to negotiate and persuade, and should use the BATNA to compare with any offer in the negotiation, to determine whether the offer is one that could be accepted.

There are some situations in which it would make sense to disclose your BATNA in a negotiation. If the other side believes that your BATNA is worse than it is, and if you are about to end the negotiation, you may want to disclose your BATNA before walking out in case the other side can come up with something that is better than your BATNA. The danger of disclosing your BATNA too early, however, is that, once you disclose it, the other side knows that he or she will only have to offer something slightly better than your BATNA and you will be better off accepting the offer, even if it is not fair.

In mediation, one of the biggest mistakes that disputants make is to compare what is being offered to what they believe is the perfect and fair solution. Unfortunately, that is not the appropriate test. The question that each disputant must ask himself or herself when assessing an offer from the other disputant is whether the offer is better or worse than his or her BATNA. If the offer is not as good as the BATNA, the disputant should reject the offer, even if the negotiators have worked hard, like each other and want a good relationship. If, on the other hand, the other side's best offer is better than the disputant's BATNA, the disputant should accept it, even if he or she does not like the other person, doesn't really like the result or believes the other person is being unfair or unreasonable.

When each disputant's BATNA is going to court (as it often is in disputes where litigation has commenced), the task of comparing an offer to the BATNA is a difficult one. As stated earlier, the outcome of litigation is somewhat unpredictable. Lawyers will have to make their best assessment of the likely outcome of litigation and consider the cost of litigation, the time it will take to complete the litigation process, the impact of the litigation on the disputant's life and the other factors that move people to settle lawsuits.

3.3.2   Interests

The second of the seven elements is interests. Interests are the wants, needs, desires and goals behind the positions taken by disputants in a negotiation. Interests can be satisfied in many ways; positions can only be satisfied in one way.

In most negotiations and mediations, both sides start by proposing the answer: their position. Only after they have decided on the answer (their position) are they prepared to talk about their concerns and the other side's concerns. Principled negotiation recommends starting with interests before coming up with the answer. After all of the interests have been established, the disputants can explore the options that may satisfy the interests.

There are a number of ways to establish the interests in a negotiation or a mediation. Asking 'why' is one example of how a person can determine the other person's interests. When people explain why their position is good for them and how it will make them better off, they are expressing their interests.

Other questions that may help uncover interests include: 'How will you be better off if your position is accepted?'; 'What were you hoping to achieve when you entered into this arrangement?'; and 'What do you hope you will be doing in five years?' The answers to these questions will often provide clues about the person's interests.

When we were purchasing our house, our interests were in buying a house that had enough room for our family, having a location that made it convenient to take our children to school, and having space for our children to play outdoors.

Positions can only be satisfied in one way; interests can be satisfied in many ways. Our interest in buying a house that made it convenient for our children to go to school could be met by buying a house within walking distance of the school, or by buying a house in an area where there was a bus or a car pool to the school. Similarly, our interest in having space for the children to play outdoors could be met by having a large garden or having a house near a park.

Focusing on interests rather than positions is the hallmark of principled negotiation and 'interest-based mediation'. A key goal in the mediation process is to uncover underlying interests so as to find a way to meet those interests by coming up with options.

3.3.3   Options

Alternatives are the different courses of action that people can undertake if they do not reach an agreement with the other disputants; options are the agreements that the disputants can reach on consent with each other's co-operation.

Once the interests have been uncovered, the task in the principled negotiation or interest-based mediation is to determine the different options that may be possible. Interests can be met in different ways, and options are the possible ways that the interests can be met.

The people in the dispute can participate in a brainstorming exercise to come up with as many options as possible that may satisfy their interests. There are usually two rules for brainstorming: no commitment; and no criticism.

Options are not offers; they are merely options. The first rule of brainstorming therefore involves separating the creativity of the brainstorming process from the commitment to a particular option. The person who comes up with an option need not be committed to it and, in fact, may think it is bad or unworkable. If people are free to brainstorm without fear that they will bind themselves to something they later regret, they are more likely to come up with creative options.

The second ground rule is that options should not be criticised while they are being generated. The brainstorming process should involve coming up with good, bad and even ridiculous options that may satisfy interests. While options are being generated, the people who are brainstorming should not be permitted to criticise the options or indicate which options they may or may not accept. There is ample time for criticism of options later in the process.

The goal of generating bad or even ridiculous options is to have as many options as possible to discuss. Discussions about seemingly unworkable options may lead to fruitful discussions about viable options.

When we were trying to purchase our new house, we had already sold our old house to a builder who was going to knock down the house and build a new one. After we had sold, my wife noticed that our built-in cupboards would fit nicely into the cupboards of the house that we wanted to purchase. The contract for the sale of our old house stated clearly that the purchaser of our old house owned the cupboard units since they were built into the house.

I telephoned the purchaser and asked whether he would consider options that might allow us to take the cupboards with us. The builder told me that he did not need the cupboards but that he did not want to give them to us for free, and he suggested a price that he thought was fair. As I was not keen to pay for the cupboards (or reduce the price that we would receive for the house), I asked whether he could think of any other options that might work. I suggested that we both consider options, even if apparently crazy, to see if we could come up with something creative that would work for him and me.

He thought for a while and then mentioned that he was planning to try and sell the house that he was going to build on our property, and that he was also planning to put a sign on our front lawn with a drawing of the home he planned to build. He could not erect the sign until he owned the house.

I suggested to him that I would allow him to put a sign on our lawn immediately if he would allow me to keep our built-in cupboards. He agreed. We used the brainstorming process to come up with an option that met both of our interests.

3.3.4 Legitimacy

Once all of the options have been brainstormed, there remains the task of sorting through them so that there can be fruitful discussions about which ones are viable.

People in a negotiation are looking to protect themselves; no one wants to be taken advantage of. One way to prevent people from feeling that they are being taken advantage of is to refer to legitimacy, benchmarks, objective criteria or standards of fairness. These are standards that one can apply to the options being considered. If there is a standard that treats everyone fairly, people are more likely to accept an option that is consistent with that standard.

Any offer proposed by the other side can be tested using objective criteria to determine whether it is fair. Principled negotiators do not reject proposals out of hand, but rather ask for justification or criteria to assess the fairness of the offer.

When my wife and I started our negotiation to purchase the house that was our first choice, we asked the vendor's agent the asking price, and were told that it was £350,000. We asked how the vendor arrived at that figure and told her that we were open to be persuaded that £350,000 was a fair price for the house. The agent said that she had asked a number of valuers to assess the value of the house and that £350,000 was the lowest of all of the appraisals.

We had done our own research and had learned that a similar house to the one that we wanted to purchase (on the same street) had sold two weeks previously for £280,000. We asked the agent why all of the valuers thought that this house was worth at least £70,000 more than that one. The agent told us that she had asked the valuers to value this house before the other house had sold. The agent then asked us if we wanted to make an offer on the house and we said that we did, for a price of £280,000. We told the agent that the reason we chose this figure was that the house down the street had sold for that amount. We based our offer on an objective criterion.

The agent took our offer to her client, and returned with a counter-offer of £300,000. Rather than rejecting the offer, we again assured the agent that we were open to be persuaded and asked her how she arrived at the figure of £300,000. She said that she had just learned that a similar house, around the corner from the one we wanted to purchase, had sold two days earlier for £300,000. We checked and her information was accurate.

We each therefore had found houses that were comparable to the one that we were trying to value. My wife and I thought the better comparison was the one on the same street, and the agent thought the better comparison was the one sold two days earlier. My wife and I suggested to the agent that we split the difference between the two prices and the agent agreed to the sale at £290,000.

We did not split the difference between two arbitrary numbers; we split the difference between objective criteria. We had searched for standards of legitimacy to protect ourselves from being taken advantage of and to persuade.

3.3.5 Communication

Negotiation and mediation are simply forums in which communication occurs. The more effective the communication, the more likely the disputants will find a solution to the issues in dispute.

People who are trying to persuade other disputants (in a negotiation or mediation) want to communicate in an effective and persuasive way. They want others to listen and, rather than reject ideas outright, they want others to consider the ideas, ask questions and genuinely explore whether the proposed solution is workable. How can one disputant expect the other to be open to ideas, open to persuasion and to consider ideas seriously, if that disputant is not prepared to offer the other disputant the same courtesy?

Effective negotiators adopt the behaviour that they want others to exhibit. If they want others to be open to persuasion, they must be open to persuasion by others; if they do not want others always to find fault with their ideas and options, they must not always find fault with options that others propose.

This is not to suggest that effective negotiators immediately accept everything that others propose. Far from it. They question, challenge and only accept if they are persuaded. They do not, however, reject others' ideas out of hand. They show themselves to be open to being persuaded and are willing to discuss any option.

When the estate agent told us that her valuers had valued the house that we wanted to buy at £350,000, we indicated that we were open to be persuaded that the house was worth £70,000 more than the one that had sold two weeks before. It may have been that the house we wanted had a new roof and the other house had an old one; it may have been that the house we wanted had a new boiler and the other house had an old one. We were open to be persuaded that there were justifiable reasons why there was a £70,000 price differential. When it turned out that there were no objective reasons for the difference, we indicated that we were prepared to pay £280,000, but were still open to be persuaded that our offer was not fair. When we learned of objective criteria justifying the £300,000 price, we were persuaded to pay more than £280,000.

There are two aspects to communication: speaking; and listening. Most advocates focus their attention on speaking, often forgetting the importance of listening. In a mediation, advocates want the other side to listen, to try to understand what they are saying, and to consider points rather than rejecting them out of hand. To encourage others to listen, effective advocates adopt the behaviour that they want others to exhibit.

The most effective advocates and communicators are interactive listeners. Interactive listeners show others that they are being heard, being listened to, by interacting with them. Interactive listening is unconditionally constructive. It cannot hurt the listener, and it can certainly help. Techniques of interactive listening include paraphrasing, using open body language, asking clarifying questions and acknowledging emotions. Interactive listening is easy when the other person says something innocuous; it is difficult when the other person says something is ridiculous, is wrong or expresses strong emotion.

There are three ways in which interactive listening can help in resolving a dispute. First, people may not have understood each other. Communication difficulties occur all the time as one disputant does not hear what the other intends to communicate. Interactive listening can clarify misunderstandings. Secondly, disputes often create a cycle of repetition and escalation. People believe that what they are saying is important, so they say it repeatedly, hoping the other person will hear and understand. Unfortunately, this often results in each person repeating arguments. Interactive listening stops the cycle of repetition because each person feels heard, and therefore doesn't feel the need to repeat. Thirdly, people like to hear their own arguments. Interactive listening improves the relationship between disputants. Interactive listening will be discussed in more detail in Chapter 7, 'Determining Interests'.

3.3.6   Relationship

The most persuasive negotiators are soft on the people in a dispute and hard on the problem.[4] While the two negotiators should be competitive in attacking the problem, they should co-operate with each other.

Disputants commonly have relationships that continue beyond the bargaining table. People encounter each other again and again over the years. It's a rare negotiation that offers no chance of the disputants seeing each other again. The most effective negotiators therefore act with an eye to the future, to implementation and to the next set of negotiations.

Being soft on the people and hard on the problem does not mean ignoring the people issues: the people issues must be addressed. But a good relationship does not equate to substantive concessions. Mediation participants can talk about the people issues, the emotions, the personal attacks and separate those discussions from the problem solving of the substantive issues.

3.3.7   Commitment

The final element of principled negotiation is commitment. As stated earlier, people in a dispute often commit first (take a position), before all of the interests have been identified, before the options have been generated and explored, and before standards of legitimacy have been applied. In principled negotiation and an interest-based mediation, commitment comes at the end of the process, not at the beginning.

Each side in a dispute should only commit to a solution if that solution is better than its BATNA. At the end of the negotiation or mediation, each side should look at its BATNA to see if the BATNA is better or worse than the option on the table. If the option is worse, the disputant should go with the BATNA; if the option is better, the disputant should commit to what is on the table.

3.4   THE CHALLENGE FOR THE MEDIATOR

The seven elements are not just ideas: they are tools that disputants and lawyers can use in the negotiation (and consequently the mediation) process. The challenge for the mediator is to determine whether the disputants are negotiating using the seven elements and, if not, how the process can be changed so that they can have a more effective negotiation.

Most people enter mediations with a competitive approach, wanting to win the negotiation or believing that they know the fair solution; this approach often leads to a stalemate. They therefore turn to the mediator. The challenge for the mediator is to convert what would otherwise be a positional competitive negotiation into a

---

4   Fisher, Ury and Patton, *op cit*, fn 1.

principled one. Just as disputants and their advocates should adopt the behaviour they want others to exhibit, the mediator will attempt to adopt the behaviour that he or she would like the disputants (and their lawyers) to exhibit. The mediator will therefore try to remain calm, will try to be open to ideas about either the process or the substance, and will try to look at the dispute as a problem to be solved rather than a battle to be won or lost. The mediator will try to remain confident that a settlement will result, and will focus on successes and agreements (even small ones) to try to create momentum toward settlement.

Finally, the mediator will attempt to listen as he or she would want the disputants to listen. The mediator will use interactive listening techniques to try to understand what is being said, in terms of the words being used, the emotions being expressed and the values being presented.

Mediation is focused on the future rather than the past. While there is obvious value in talking about and exploring what has occurred to bring the disputants to the table, the focus of the process really is on attempting to determine whether there is anything that the disputants can do that makes more sense for both of them than going forward with their respective BATNAs.

Tips for Lawyers

- You have the opportunity to take a competitive approach, a co-operative approach or a principled approach to negotiating in a mediation. While there may be situations where competitive or co-operative bargaining is appropriate, you will often best serve your client by adopting the seven elements of principled negotiation (alternatives, interests, options, legitimacy, relationship, communication and commitment). If you decide to take the principled negotiation approach, you may want to use the elements to prepare yourself (and your client) for the negotiation.

- In preparing your client, you will want to identify and explore your client's alternatives, the things your client can do completely independently of the other person in the negotiation. Your client will need to determine his or her best alternative (BATNA), whether it is going to court or something else. Next, you will need to determine your client's interests and take an educated guess at the other side's interests. Then brainstorm with your client to discover the different options that may satisfy the interests. Look for standards of legitimacy or objective criteria that may persuade the other side. Create a strategy for your communication in the negotiation: what are you and your client going to say and how will you say it?

- Think about your client's relationship with the other client and the ways in which they may or may not work together in the future. Finally, make sure that your client has the authority to make the relevant commitment at the mediation (or at least has access to the person who has authority).

- At the mediation itself, you can use the seven elements to keep you and your client focused. Your client need only agree to a deal if it is better than his or her BATNA. Stay focused on satisfying your client's interests and try to determine whether you accurately predicted the other side's interests. Try to be open to creative options that are raised in the mediation.

- Encourage the other person to refer to standards of legitimacy or objective criteria. If they put forward a number, ask why they came up with that number and not a different number. Force them to justify their proposal and be prepared to justify yours.

- Try to communicate in a way that accomplishes your client's objectives, and helps maintain or improve the relationship. At the end of the mediation, your client must decide whether to make a commitment to an option and should only do so if that option is better than the BATNA (usually going to court).

- Try in a mediation to adopt the behaviour that you want the other side to exhibit. You may want to be open to persuasion so that the other side will be open to persuasion; you may want to express your interests to encourage the other side to present theirs; you may want to listen interactively so that the other side will listen to you.

Tips for Mediators

- Some disputants will approach mediation with a competitive mindset, trying to out-think and out-manoeuvre the other disputant in the negotiation. If so, your challenge will be to keep the process moving and to allow those disputants to see the benefits of taking a more principled approach.

- You will need to ask them questions to uncover the interests behind their positions, so that you can help them come up with a solution that satisfies their interests. You will need to encourage them to be creative in the brainstorming of options, and help them focus on standards of legitimacy rather than on what they 'want'.

- You may need to reframe comments that are made so that they are understood and do not damage the disputants' relationship. At the end of the mediation, you will probably be encouraging them to commit to an option if that option is better than their BATNA.

- The process of mediation belongs to the disputants, not to the mediator. That being said, if you can transform a competitive negotiation into a principled one, you will have significantly increased the likelihood that the disputants will resolve their dispute.

CHAPTER 4

BEFORE THE MEDIATION

If we think mediation is a good thing, where do we start? How do we get others to agree to mediate? How do we find the right mediator? What if the disputants do not agree on their choice of mediator? Should there be one mediator or two? How do we check for conflicts of interest? What documents are signed before the mediation and what do they say? How much written material should a mediator get before the mediation? How should disputants and lawyers prepare for mediation? Who should attend the mediation? Should the disputants meet privately with the mediator before the mediation begins? What about the logistics – who books the rooms, arranges for food?

These are all important questions that must be considered before the mediation begins.

4.1   HOW DOES AN ISSUE GET TO MEDIATION?

There are three common ways for an issue to get to mediation. The first is that a statute requires that the mediation occur. In a number of jurisdictions, mediation is a mandatory step in the process of resolving a dispute and a law is drafted that requires disputants to attend a mediation.[1]

A dispute can also get to mediation where the disputants are parties to a contract that mandates mediation. Some people, when they enter into a contract, have a clause in the contract that sets out that, in case of a dispute about the interpretation of the contract, the disputants should proceed to mediation before proceeding to arbitration or court.

The third way that a dispute gets to mediation is consensually. Both sides may agree that mediation makes sense in the circumstances and voluntarily agree to participate in the mediation process.

4.2   WHAT IF ONLY ONE SIDE WANTS TO MEDIATE?

Sometimes one side believes that mediation makes sense while the other side believes that it is not a good idea. It is left to the disputant (or his or her lawyer) to persuade the other side to attend the mediation. How is it best to persuade them?

A common approach to trying to persuade others is to explain the benefits of mediation and the reasons why it would be a mistake for both sides not to attend. Unfortunately, most people don't like being told that they should do something, even if it is a good thing. They may instinctively react against it, assuming that it must be a bad idea if the other side wants it.

---

1   For a full examination of mandatory mediation, see Brazil, WD, 'Court ADR 25 Years After Pound: Have We Found A Better Way?' (2002) 18 Ohio St J on Disp Resol 93.

A different persuasive approach would be to use all of the options, including the option that mediation is not appropriate in the particular case. By demonstrating an openness to ideas that are not your first choice, you would be adopting the behaviour that you want others to exhibit.

Some lawyers ask the mediator to try to persuade the other side to attend a mediation, assuming that, if the request comes from someone neutral, it is more likely to be accepted. Most mediators will assume the responsibility of trying to persuade people to attend mediations. Like disputants and their lawyers, mediators who demonstrate that they are open to be persuaded can sometimes persuade reluctant people to attend the mediation.

4.3   SELECTING THE MEDIATOR

How does one choose the best and most appropriate mediator for the situation? There is no scientific method for selecting a mediator. The most common method is to select a mediator who has been referred by a colleague. Also, there are a number of ADR organisations that have lists of qualified mediators. These organisations can provide lists of potential neutrals, and their curriculum vitae, so that disputants can make an informed decision when selecting mediators.[2]

In determining which mediator to select, a disputant should consider issues such as the amount of experience the mediator has mediating these types of disputes, the mediator's fees, the mediator's availability and the mediator's approach (whether the mediator considers himself or herself facilitative, evaluative or transformative).

Some organisations have created designations to assist disputants in assessing the qualifications of mediators. For example, the ADR Institute of Canada has created the Chartered Mediator (CMed designation), which can be used to assist people in selecting mediators. A CMed is a mediator who has significant training in mediation, has mediation experience and has successfully completed a skills assessment. While a CMed is not a guarantee of quality (just as inclusion of a mediator on a roster is not an assurance of quality), a CMed is an indication of significant training and experience, and of at least a minimum level of skill.[3]

One of the issues that disputants will want to consider when selecting a mediator is the degree of substantive expertise required to mediate the dispute effectively. Some disputants feel more comfortable when the mediator is an expert in the subject area of the dispute. They select the mediator because of that person's background in the field.

It is more important for an evaluative mediator to be a subject-matter expert than it is for a facilitative mediator. Because an evaluative mediator will be assessing the arguments presented by each side, he or she will need to understand to a significant degree the issues that are being raised by the disputants.

---

2   Our company, the Stitt Feld Handy Group, is an example of a private provider of mediators. In the UK, ADR Chambers UK and Centre for Effective Dispute Resolution (CEDR) are examples of groups that provide lists of mediators. ADR Chambers has a roster of retired Law Lords, judges and prominent lawyers who provide mediation services and CEDR has a roster of qualified lawyer and non-lawyer mediators.

3   As of the writing of this book, the Chartered Institute of Arbitrators is also considering introducing a CMed designation to the UK.

Most people in the mediation community believe that the mediator need not be an expert on the substance in order to mediate effectively. The mediator will never know as much as the disputants and their lawyers know about the issues in dispute. The mediator does need to be a process expert, understanding how to help disputants and lawyers solve apparently unsolvable problems. The fact that the mediator is not a subject-matter expert can sometimes even help, as the mediator may not be encumbered by traditional approaches to a problem and may be more likely to help the disputants think 'outside the box' in coming up with a solution.

At the same time, the mediator will need to understand the issues in dispute well enough to be able to communicate effectively with the disputants during the mediation. It would usually not be a good use of the disputants' time to explain basic concepts to the mediator.

For example, when selecting a mediator for a construction dispute, disputants would be wise to choose a mediator who is familiar with construction issues, and is also a good mediator. The mediator need not necessarily be a contractor, an architect or a construction lawyer, provided the mediator is familiar with the terms used and the general issues raised by the dispute.

What if the disputants cannot agree on the identity of the mediator? If the disputants cannot agree, many ADR organisations will recommend a particular mediator, depending on the issue and amount in dispute. Alternatively, an ADR organisation can provide disputants with a list of names of potential mediators. The disputants can then rank the mediators in their order of preference. The mediator with the highest total ranking who is available to act will then be appointed. If the disputants cannot agree on the process for selecting a mediator and are required to mediate by statute, the statute will usually provide for the appointment of a mediator. If the disputants are going to mediation because a contract requires them to mediate and they cannot agree on their choice of mediator, they can usually go to court and have a court choose a mediator for them.

Does a mediator need to have legal knowledge or need to be a lawyer to mediate? The answer, I believe, is that it depends on the issue being mediated. If the issue is in the context of litigation and is a legal issue, someone without legal training may not have the necessary experience to be able to assist the disputants to work through the issue.

On the other hand, there are many issues that need to be mediated, whether or not in the context of litigation, that are not legal. Those disputes do not require a lawyer-mediator. For neighbourhood disputes or disputes among members of a board of directors, for example, there would be no need for the mediator to be a lawyer. Where the issue is one that is complex and not legal, it may be more important to have someone mediate who has expertise other than law. For example, if the dispute concerns the appropriate accounting rules to apply, it may be best to retain an accountant; if the dispute relates to the development of computer software, it may make sense to have a mediator who is familiar with software development.

4.4   CONFLICT OF INTEREST

Suppose a mediator has an interest in the outcome of the dispute. Say, for example, a dispute relates to whether a public company has an obligation to make a large payment and the mediator is a shareholder in the public company. Or say the dispute relates to a damages claim by a woman who was wearing a fur coat and had paint thrown on her by an environmentalist, and say the mediator is a card-carrying member of Greenpeace who does not believe in using animal fur to make coats. Does the mediator have to disclose the potential conflict in either or both of these situations? Suppose the mediator believes that he or she can put the potential conflict out of his or her mind. Does that make it alright to proceed without disclosing?

Where a mediator has an interest in the outcome of the dispute, there is, a potential conflict of interest, and there is a potential conflict in both of the preceding examples. My recommendation to the mediator is to disclose the possibility of the existence of a conflict, as soon as the mediator becomes aware of it, to allow the disputants to consider their course of action. If at least one of the disputants prefers for the mediator not to act, the mediator should not mediate.

On the other hand, if both (or all) disputants waive the conflict (that is, agree to proceed with the mediation notwithstanding the conflict), the mediation may continue provided the disputants waive the conflict voluntarily and with full information.[4] The mediator is not the decision-maker in a mediation; that role is left for the disputants. The mediator merely assists the disputants to negotiate and to come up with creative options that may overcome obstacles. The mediator does not have the power to decide. If the mediation is an evaluative one, the issue of conflict could be more significant than it is for a facilitative mediation.

That being said, some mediators are uncomfortable acting, even when the disputants consent, when there is a conflict of interest. Mediators who are uncomfortable should not act.

4.5   ONE MEDIATOR OR TWO?

Although most mediations are conducted by sole mediators, an increasing number are being co-mediated (conducted by two mediators). Co-mediations sometimes occur where an experienced mediator is mentoring a less experienced mediator (in which case the junior mediator will play a minor role). At other times, however, a second mediator can be helpful (and sometimes necessary) because of the complexity of the issues or the number of participants. Sometimes two mediators are used because one has process expertise (is a good mediator) and the other has substantive expertise (is the subject-matter expert).

There are numerous advantages to co-mediation, if the disputants can afford the extra cost. Mediators will have different experiences and can bring different yet complementary expertise to the mediation. For example, where there are financial and legal issues, one mediator could have accounting experience and the other could have a legal background.

---

4   I should note that there are some Codes of Conduct such as the Civil/Commercial Mediation Code of Practice from The Law Society (UK) and Ontario (Canada) Bar Association Code that prohibit a mediator from acting if there is a conflict. The UK Code does allow the mediator to act in the case of consent.

One disputant may feel uncomfortable with a particular mediator, for any of a number of reasons. Having two mediators increases the likelihood that all of the disputants will have at least one mediator with whom they feel comfortable and in whom they can confide. It may be possible to match characteristics of the mediator to characteristics of the disputants, to increase comfort further. For example, in a dispute between a man and a woman with gender issues, the disputants may be more comfortable if there is a man and a woman mediator.

One mediator can play a facilitative role in the mediation while the other can play an evaluative role. I have brought along to mediations an experienced and well-respected lawyer as a co-mediator. He does not participate greatly in the early stages of the mediation. As we near the end of the process, if the disputants cannot agree on the answer to a legal question, he becomes more involved.

The experienced mediator provides his insights and views about the issues raised in the mediation. While he does not tell the disputants what 'would' happen in court (since the outcome is inherently unpredictable), he does provide guidance on how a court may view certain issues, and on how a court might test disputants' credibility. He also gives the disputants a sense of how a neutral person looking at the issues for the first time might assess them. While a sole mediator can talk about the likely outcome at trial and provide an opinion (evaluate the dispute), the impact is sometimes greater if the mediator who provides the guidance has not participated in the mediation to that point and has the experience to provide helpful insights to the disputants.

It Happened at Mediation

I was mediating a dispute between a franchisor and a former franchisee about an alleged breach of the franchise agreement. The franchisor alleged that the franchisee had not operated the franchise in accordance with the training provided to franchisees and, therefore, pursuant to the franchise agreement, the franchisor had the right to take back the franchise from the franchisee without compensation.

My co-mediator, an experienced lawyer and business person, listened attentively as I mediated the dispute. Late in the mediation, we were in caucus (a private meeting) with the franchisor who was explaining how the language of the contract was clear and how a court could only find in the franchisor's favour. My co-mediator chose this moment to express his concerns about the franchisor's case. He told the franchisor's lawyer that, while the contract was clear, no one could predict what a court would do. The franchisee was a poor person who had spent a lot of money on the franchise, and had lost his life's savings in the endeavour. My co-mediator suggested that a court might focus more on the amount of training and supervision provided to the franchisee than on the wording of the contract. He reminded the franchisor that, while courts apply the law, judges are human. The franchisee came across as sympathetic and unsophisticated, and a court might fight for a way to give the franchisee his franchise fee back.

The franchisor considered the comments made by my co-mediator, and amended his views on the type of settlement he was prepared to accept in the mediation.

Two mediators can divide tasks and the mediation can therefore proceed faster. For example, one mediator may facilitate discussions while the other takes notes, or one mediator may have a private discussion (a caucus) with one side while the other mediator caucuses with the other side.

A second mediator can help keep track of all of the information that has been presented. There is often a lot of material presented at mediation and it is not always possible for one mediator to keep track of all that has been said and done.

Two heads are better than one. A second mediator may see an opportunity that the first has missed. In the stage of the mediation where creative options are being developed, both mediators may participate in the brainstorming process and may be more likely than a single mediator to come up with a good creative option. Finally, and perhaps most importantly, one mediator can jump in to help the other if the first mediator falters.

It Happened at Mediation

My partner Frank Handy and I were mediating a dispute between a group of suppliers and a group of purchasers who were attempting to set up a process to conduct future negotiations. Legislation required them to negotiate with each other about the terms of the purchase and sale of the goods, and if they could not agree, they were required to participate in an arbitration process. The mediation took place over a weekend at a resort so that there would be no distractions. On Saturday night, Frank and I worked feverishly with the purchasers to fine-tune one of the options so that it would be satisfactory to the suppliers. We worked late into the night, and we believed we had come up with a creative way to satisfy all of the suppliers' interests. I was anxious to present the idea the next morning, expecting the suppliers to compliment us on our ingenuity and hard work.

The suppliers' response was, to say the least, not what I expected. The leader of the supplier group swore at me, ridiculed the option and complained about his frustration that we had completely missed what it was that was important to them. I was shocked. I had no idea what to say or how to respond.

Fortunately, Frank was not as enamoured with the proposal as I, and was not caught off guard. While I froze, he was able to ask the group what its concerns were with the proposal and how the proposal could be revised to meet the group's interests and still meet the other side's interests. Having a second mediator who could be objective and react when I was in trouble was invaluable.

There are some potential difficulties with co-mediation. The most obvious disadvantage is that hiring two mediators is usually more expensive than hiring one mediator (though this is not always the case when the second mediator is less experienced).

Another difficulty can occur when the mediators differ about how to proceed and differ on the direction that they believe the mediation should take. When the mediators differ, they may need to call a mediator caucus to discuss concerns, or they may discuss the issue in front of and with the disputants, asking for the disputants' input and trying to adopt appropriate dispute resolution behaviour.

The co-mediators may also struggle if they are not used to mediating together in terms of knowing when each person should speak, when to caucus and when to intervene. The mediators may need to develop signals for each other so that transitions can be smooth.

4.6 THE AGREEMENT TO MEDIATE

Most mediators will send an agreement to mediate to the disputants in advance of the mediation, and ask the disputants and their lawyers to sign and return the agreement. A sample agreement can be found at Appendix A. The Agreement to Mediate covers issues such as the confidentiality of the process, the timing of the mediation, the mediator's fees, the agreement of the disputants not to call the mediator as a witness, and the without prejudice nature of the process.

4.7 PREPARING FOR MEDIATION

4.7.1 Written material

How much written material is ideal for the mediator before the mediation? Mediators differ. Some want to see everything, to be as well 'prepared' as possible. Others want only a short synopsis of the dispute. Others still want no material, believing that they are process experts, not substantive experts.

Most mediators want enough information to be able to understand the issues in dispute, but not so much that they are overwhelmed. They will usually ask disputants to provide to them, prior to the mediation, a summary of the facts, the issues in dispute and the disputants' perspectives on the dispute.

How much time should disputants and lawyers spend preparing material? Some lawyers spend a significant amount of time preparing material; others spend little time, believing that their persuasiveness at mediation will not be affected by the quality of their written material (or lack thereof).

I cannot overstate the importance of lawyers preparing quality material. Time spent preparing written material for the mediation will be rewarded with a better result. This is not to suggest that longer material is better than shorter material. The best mediation briefs I have received were between five and ten pages, but were extremely persuasive.

I would recommend that the material in the briefs should present, as persuasively as possible, the strongest case for that side. Some lawyers and mediators worry that aggressive briefs set an adversarial tone for the mediation and therefore inhibit co-operation and prevent settlement. I have found, on the other hand, that an aggressive mediation brief that presents the legal case in the strongest possible terms is not only appropriate, it is also helpful.

That is not to suggest that the mediation brief should set out positions and insist that the other side accept those positions or even suggest that a court will accept the arguments. The brief should make clear that facts will need to be proven at trial and no one can state conclusively what will or will not be proven at trial. The brief should present, in the strongest possible terms, what would be argued if the case were to go to trial. It should then recognise that trial is unpredictable and that a settlement on appropriate terms would make more sense than going to court and state an openness to explore settlement possibilities. The mediation can then focus on the solutions that avoid recourse to the courts.

The purpose of the mediation (and the mediation brief) is not to persuade the mediator, it is to persuade the other side. The brief should not dwell on facts that the other side knows. It should focus on facts and arguments that are likely to be presented at trial.

There are situations, however, in which the mediation briefs are focused on persuading the mediator and are given to the mediator in confidence. Where, for example, one disputant has information that he or she wants to share with the mediator, but does not want to share with the other side, the disputant may request that the briefs not be exchanged. Confidential information could include undisclosed evidence that might be used at trial or business plans that are confidential for competitive reasons. In other situations, a disputant may ask to submit a confidential brief where that disputant wants to settle the dispute and believes that the brief will unnecessarily antagonise the other disputant.

Confidential briefs are relatively rare, however, because they do not usually help accomplish the goal of mediation – that is, to try to settle the dispute. If the primary reason for presenting cogent arguments in a brief is to persuade the other disputant and open the door to possible settlement options, that goal is not achieved with confidential briefs. When disputants have confidential information that they feel they need to disclose to the mediator, they can still draft and exchange persuasive briefs, and can disclose the confidential information in private caucuses during the mediation. If a disputant believes that his or her brief would unnecessarily antagonise, the disputant can usually tone down the brief and use a conciliatory tone.

How many documents should each side give to the mediator to read? Some lawyers provide the mediator with copies of many documents, while others are selective. It is usually neither effective nor necessary to include numerous documents in the mediation brief, unless the other side is unaware of the documents and could be persuaded by them. There are usually few documents that are necessary for the mediator to be able to understand the issues in dispute and mediate effectively, and only those key documents should be included.

4.7.2   Other preparation

In addition to written material, how else should a lawyer prepare for mediation? The lawyer will want to meet with his or her client before the mediation to prepare the client for the process and make sure that the client knows what to expect, what to say, and what not to say. One way to prepare is to use the seven elements presented in detail in Chapter 3, 'Mediation: Facilitated Negotiation'. Through that preparation, the client will understand the strengths and weaknesses of the case, what will happen if no agreement is reached, and what creative solutions might be possible. The client will also gain a sense of what should and should not be disclosed.

The lawyer will also want to review the mediation agreement with the client and make sure the client understands the mediation process, particularly the significance of the fact that the process is without prejudice.

How can the lawyer help his or her client get into the other side's head, to really know what the other disputant is thinking and where he or she is coming from? Before attempting to change someone's mind, a disputant has to understand how the other person perceives the problem and what solutions seem to make sense to him or her. The lawyer may therefore want the client to participate in a role-reversal exercise, where the client pretends to be the opposing disputant with the goal of finding out more about how the other person understands the dispute.

The lawyer and the client may even role-play the mediation itself so that the client (and lawyer) can practise what is going to be said, and think how to respond to what others will be saying. Lawyers see the benefit of practising their submissions for court but sometimes forget to practise the equally important submissions they will make at mediation.

The lawyer may also need to do some preparation without the client. The lawyer will want to prepare what will be said in the storytelling stage of the mediation (discussed in Chapter 6, 'Storytelling'). The lawyer will want to make sure he or she has a clear understanding of all of the legal and factual issues in dispute, and the position that each side has taken on those issues. If any settlement offers have been made, the lawyer will want to review those offers and be familiar with them, even if they have been withdrawn.

The lawyer may also want to spend time thinking about some creative options that may help resolve some of the more contentious issues in the litigation. What might the client be prepared to consider in terms of a creative solution to the problem?

You will notice that I have not recommended that either the lawyer or the client spend time thinking about an initial position or a bottom line in the negotiation process. Coming up with 'the' answer before the mediation starts can be counter-productive and unhelpful. Through the mediation process, the client and lawyer can decide what is an acceptable option and what is not acceptable.

That said, it is likely that there will come a point in the mediation where the disputant will be asked to submit an offer for settlement to the other side, and it would be useful for the lawyer and the client to think about what the proposal might be, and be flexible to change based on what is said in the mediation.

4.8   WHO SHOULD ATTEND THE MEDIATION?

Often it is obvious who should attend a mediation: those involved in the dispute. Sometimes, though, it is not so clear. For example, who should represent a company: the person who has information about the dispute or the person with authority to settle? When should friends attend to support those who have a dispute? Should lawyers always attend? Should anyone else attend?

As you may suspect, there are no clear answers to any of these questions. As for the appropriate representative (or representatives) from a company, the ideal situation is for both the person with information about the dispute and the person with authority to settle the dispute to attend. Often that is one person, though sometimes it is two. If a choice between the two must be made, the more important person at the mediation is the person with authority.

As for when friends and confidants should attend, they should attend if the disputant needs their input in order to agree to a deal. If a friend would provide moral support and make one of the disputants more comfortable (but is not absolutely necessary to resolving the dispute), I tend to err on the side of encouraging the disputant on the other side to allow the friend to attend, though other mediators try to keep them out. These mediators believe that more people prolong the process and create obstacles to settlement. I have a concern that if a disputant asks for someone to attend and the mediator discourages attendance, the disputant may be less confident, less comfortable with the mediator and less likely to confide in the mediator.

As for whether lawyers should attend, my view is that they should obviously attend if litigation has commenced, and should probably attend if litigation is contemplated or if the dispute relates to legal issues. The matter is less clear when the issue is not a legal one (such as a dispute between co-workers or a dispute among a board of directors). Even in those cases, however, lawyers have expertise and creativity, and can add great value to the process. Each case must be examined independently to determine whether the extra cost for the lawyer would be justified.

In some mediations, experts attend to provide guidance on specific issues. I have conducted mediations where actuaries, accountants, engineers and computer experts have attended to provide expert guidance.

I have found that experts can often add great value to the mediation process.

4.9   GETTING READY TO MEDIATE

4.9.1   Preliminary meetings

Should mediators have preliminary meetings with disputants before the mediation, to give them an opportunity to speak to the mediator without the other disputant present? Those who use preliminary meetings believe they make sense for a number of reasons.

First, they provide disputants with an opportunity to vent their feelings. While venting feelings can occur in the presence of the other disputant, it may not be as vociferous or as direct. People may hold back if the other disputant is present. As will be discussed later, people sometimes have a need to tell someone their problems before they can focus on solving them.

Secondly, preliminary meetings familiarise mediators with the facts and help them prepare for the mediation. A mediator can get a sense of the issues in dispute, the perspective of each disputant, the willingness of disputants to participate in the mediation, and even possible avenues for settlement.

Thirdly, preliminary meetings give the mediator an opportunity to coach the disputants before they get into the room with the other side. Where there is no preliminary conference, situations can arise where disputants say things at the beginning of the mediation that are destructive and unproductive. With a little coaching, they can say the same thing in a non-destructive way so that it encourages the other disputant to think creatively, rather than causing the other disputant to react angrily.

Fourthly, preliminary meetings allow the mediator to screen for cases that are inappropriate for mediation (such as those mentioned earlier in Chapter 2, 'Why Mediate?'). If there is a threat of violence, for example, the mediator can recommend another mediator who is trained and skilled in dealing with violence cases, or can recommend a different process that is more appropriate for the dispute.

Mediators do not always have the luxury, however, of holding preliminary sessions with each of the disputants. These meetings will necessarily mean that the mediation will cost more, and it will usually mean that the mediation will take more time, often over a number of days.

Further, some mediators believe that the preliminary meetings can harm the likelihood of settlement. They believe that mediation works best when people talk to and try to persuade each other, rather than talking to and trying to persuade the mediator. When disputants work through their issues and emotions in front of each other, they may be more likely to see the other person's perspective and be more open to creative ideas. Further, they may learn how to resolve conflict with each other so that if other disputes arise, they may not need to call a mediator as they may have a process for working issues through themselves.

Also, some mediators believe that the exchange between the disputants at an emotional level is helpful. Provided the mediator facilitates the discussion in a way that does not allow the discussion to deteriorate into personal attacks, the communication between the disputants can be an important stage in the mediation process.

Sometimes mediators have no choice but to have preliminary meetings. Issues can arise so that the mediation cannot start until certain issues are resolved, and those issues can sometimes only be resolved through preliminary meetings.

It Happened at Mediation

I was mediating a dispute between a commercial landlord and tenant relating to the interpretation of a lease. The landlord was arguing that the tenant was supposed to pay for certain renovations and the tenant was arguing that the lease stipulated that the renovations were the landlord's responsibility. When I arrived at the mediation, I learned that the tenant had stopped paying rent because he believed that the landlord was not fulfilling his obligations to pay for the renovations. The landlord refused even to participate in the mediation until all arrears of rent were paid (as he considered the issues to be separate). I needed to hold preliminary meetings to help the disputants find a solution to the payment of rent issue so that they could participate in the mediation.

In my preliminary meeting with the tenant, I learned that the landlord had written to the tenant's bank about the dispute and the tenant's bank had reduced the tenant's credit limit. The tenant was angry about this and wanted to restore his credit limit. The tenant therefore agreed to provide the landlord with a cheque for the arrears of rent, in return for the landlord agreeing to write a letter to the tenant's bank recommending that the bank reinstate the tenant's prior credit limit.

In the end, the disputants had resolved all issues except who was responsible for paying an invoice of a few thousand pounds. Throughout the process, they had been open with each other about their concerns, and had discussed the fact that they both acted without consulting each other and that that had created problems for them. With respect to the outstanding invoice, they agreed that they would both pay the total invoice, and would use the extra money to take a trip together to Las Vegas, just the two of them. They believed that once they got to know each other better, they would communicate better, and future disputes were less likely to arise. I felt comfortable that the relationship had been repaired.

4.9.2   The logistics

Before the mediation commences, someone must co-ordinate schedules and find a date that is convenient to disputants and their lawyers. Who is responsible for the logistics? While this role usually goes to the mediator, it is not always so. If the mediator agrees to act as logistics co-ordinator, that can work well; otherwise, one or both of the lawyers (or their assistants) must assume the role of logistics co-ordinator.

The logistics person must find facilities that are suitable. I will deal with this aspect in more detail in the next chapter, 'Setting the Table'.

The person will also usually arrange for the disputants to send the mediator a retainer cheque for half each of the anticipated fee and disbursements of the mediation. While retainers are not always requested, they are becoming increasingly common for mediators.

Finally, the administrative person must determine who will be present at the mediation, and make sure that those attending have set aside the time necessary (whether that be three hours, one day or, for multi-disputant and multi-issue mediations, a week).

Disputes surrounding logistics are rare, but they do occur. When they arise, mediators must mediate the conflict in the same way that they would mediate any other conflict.

It Happened at Mediation

I was mediating a dispute among the members of a board of directors of an organisation. At the last meeting, there had been an acrimonious argument and some of the members of the board had walked out of the meeting. Both sides decided to mediate and asked me to speak to the two groups separately. I learned that each group was in a different hotel in downtown Toronto so, as part of arranging logistics, I asked the groups at which hotel they preferred to conduct the mediation. They each refused to be in the same hotel as the other group.

After much discussion, the groups did agree that it made more sense to be in the same hotel, but they insisted on being on different floors.

I should note that the process of working through the hotel issue was not superfluous to the mediation process; it was part of it. The disputants had now managed to work their way through an issue where they had had a disagreement and they developed a process that they used later on in the day to deal with the substantive issues. The disputants did work through their issues that day and agreed on a new process for future board meetings.

Tips for Lawyers

- If you want to bring a matter to a mediation, and there is no contract or legislation requiring this, you will need to negotiate with the other side and persuade them to participate in the mediation. The skills that you need to persuade are no different than the skills you need in the mediation itself. You will need to listen, be open to persuasion, and look for ways to satisfy interests. Be open to the possibility that mediation is not the best process for resolving the dispute.

- Take the time to select the appropriate mediator for your dispute. Find out the mediator's qualifications and approach and make sure the mediator knows enough about the subject of the dispute to be able to communicate with you. If you are using an evaluative mediator, make sure that the mediator has substantive expertise (or is a retired judge, expert in making legal determinations).

- If the mediator has a potential conflict of interest, the issue should be raised with all disputants and the mediation should only proceed on consent after full disclosure.

- For most disputes, it will not be necessary to have more than one mediator. However, it is rarely harmful to have a second mediator. If there are multiple issues and multiple disputants, you may want to consider the benefits of having two mediators.

- Spend the necessary time to prepare an effective mediation brief. Try to present, in the most effective and persuasive way, the best arguments that you would raise were the matter to proceed to trial (or arbitration). The best briefs are five to ten pages and are written in an easy to understand style. It is not usually necessary to provide a significant number of documents unless the other side is unaware of them. It can often be helpful to conclude with a statement to the effect that trial is unpredictable and that you and your client are coming to the mediation open to be persuaded and looking for a fair settlement.

- You will need to prepare your client for the mediation. Substantively, the seven elements (discussed in Chapter 3, 'Mediation: Facilitated Negotiation') can guide the preparation. Review with your client the draft Agreement to Mediate, including the fact that the mediation is without prejudice (without prejudice will be discussed in detail in the next chapter, 'Setting the Table'). You will also want to set out for your client how you anticipate the process will proceed. You may want to discuss how much talking you will do and how much your client will do, particularly in the first part of the mediation. If you have clients who are at all articulate, consider having them present their concerns, experiences and goals.

- You will need to determine whether the person attending the mediation with you has knowledge of the facts and has the authority to settle the dispute. If the person does not have authority (or if the person has limited authority), it can be helpful if the person with more authority is available by telephone.

- You will need to determine who else (in addition to the person with factual information and authority) should attend the mediation. You may, for example, consider having an expert or a friend attend.

- You will need to discuss with your client the confidentiality of the mediation. If the mediation is confidential, you will need to let your client know that he or she cannot disclose what is said in the mediation to others who did not attend. If your client needs to report to others (not in attendance at the mediation) about what has occurred, you will need to make sure that the mediator and the other disputants are aware that your client will be reporting what is said, and the limits of the reporting obligation.

- You may want to ask your client to do a role reversal and try to understand the case from the other side's perspective.

- You and your client could brainstorm some creative options that may help to resolve difficult issues. You may want to discuss with your client the possibility that brainstorming may occur in the mediation and that you may be asked to come up with options that you would not be prepared to accept (see the discussion in Chapter 9, 'Brainstorming Options').

- You need not spend a lot of time focusing on bottom lines and opening positions, as both should depend on how much your client is persuaded during the mediation. However, you should have a sense, based on the information you have, of what offer you might make to open the negotiation if you were to learn nothing that affected your thinking.

- You may need to do some research on the facts or the law so that you can make an effective opening presentation (the 'storytelling'). You may want to practice what you will say.

- You should bring to the mediation any documents that you think may be helpful (or that the other side may refer to). You may also want to bring with you a draft release (if appropriate).

Tips for Mediators

- If the disputants cannot agree on whether to proceed with mediation, you may be asked to try to persuade one of the disputants to participate in the mediation. When speaking to the person who does not want to attend the mediation, you can use the seven elements as your guide. You will need to discover why the person does not want to attend mediation (the interests), brainstorm options and, above all, be open to be persuaded that mediation is not the best option. Adopt the behaviour that you want the other person to exhibit (that is, being open to be persuaded).

- If, when reviewing the facts of the case, you determine that there may be a conflict of interest, you should bring the issue to the attention of the disputants and ask them whether they want to waive the conflict or whether they would prefer another mediator.

- If you are co-mediating, you will need to prepare with your co-mediator and discuss a number of issues:

  (1) You will need to decide how to divide your tasks. Perhaps you will want to divide 'setting the table' (discussed in the next chapter) so that each of you can be heard at the beginning of the mediation. You may decide that one of you will talk or facilitate while the other writes on the flipchart; you may decide to divide the various stages of the mediation so that you take turns leading and facilitating the discussion.

  (2) You will need to discuss how to signal to each other when one of you wants to intervene or to take a break. Some mediators write each other notes while others develop visual cues.

  (3) You will need to decide whether you want to go into private session (caucus) together or split up. If you stay together, you will both hear the same story and you will not be perceived to favour one disputant or the other. If you split up, you can save significant time and the disputants will not feel that they are being left alone for too long. A lot of co-mediators therefore decide to split up for private sessions.

  (4) In order to avoid the appearance that one mediator favours the side that he or she is meeting with, each of the co-mediators may decide to meet privately with both sides. In between, the mediators may meet with each other to discuss what they have heard and what could be presented to each side.

  (5) Co-mediators will need to discuss the mediation model that they want to use. Will the mediation be completely facilitative? Will one of the mediators use an evaluative approach? Do the mediators agree on the stages of the mediation?

- You will want to have the disputants agree to the terms of, and sign, an Agreement to Mediate before the start of the mediation.

- You will probably want to send a letter to each side, enclosing the Agreement to Mediate, asking each side to send you a written summary of their perspective on the dispute, asking who will attend the mediation, and asking for a retainer for your fees. It will probably be your job to co-ordinate schedules and find a venue.

- It is essential that you review the material that the disputants provide to you. There is nothing more frustrating for a lawyer at mediation than a mediator who has not read the material. If there are a lot of documents presented, you will need to assess which documents are important for the resolution of the dispute and review them.

- You may consider having preliminary meetings with the disputants, especially in multi-disputant disputes.

CHAPTER 5

SETTING THE TABLE

5.1   THE STAGES OF A MEDIATION

Mediations are all different and mediators conduct them with their own ideas of the best process. There is no set number of 'stages' of mediation. However, most mediators approach a mediation with an anticipated structure and maintain the flexibility to deviate from it. The model that I use involves seven stages:

(1) setting the table;

(2) storytelling;

(3) determining interests;

(4) setting out the issues;

(5) brainstorming options;

(6) selecting the durable options; and

(7) closing the mediation.

5.2   SETTING THE TABLE LITERALLY

The first task for the mediator in the mediation is to 'set the table', both literally and figuratively. As stated in the last chapter, the mediator is usually responsible for literally setting the table in the sense of making sure that the facilities are appropriate for the mediation. This includes booking the facilities and making sure there are enough rooms for the disputants to have private meetings (caucuses). Even where the mediation is set for a specific period of time, the mediator should try to arrange for facilities that are available all day in case the mediation goes on longer than expected. The mediator will need to ensure that the room in which the mediation will be conducted has a table large enough for all participants and has enough chairs. The mediator will also make sure there are refreshments, telephones in each room, paper, pens, flipchart, markers and tape.

5.3   SETTING THE TABLE FIGURATIVELY

How should the mediator start the mediation? How can mediators make the disputants comfortable, set out the process, start the disputants on the right track and yet not take so much time that everyone becomes bored or frustrated?

The mediator will usually try to set the tone for the mediation and create an atmosphere that is conducive to settlement. The mediator needs therefore to set the table figuratively as well as literally. The mediator tries to create a comfortable and positive tone for the disputants by proposing a structure that encourages the disputants to participate.

This may be the first opportunity for the disputants to meet the mediator, so the mediator will try to engender the disputants' trust and confidence in both the mediator and the mediation process. The mediator will also attempt to calm emotions and nerves, as the disputants may be anxious about how the process will unfold and what the outcome will be.

5.3.1   The introduction

How does the process start? The mediator will usually start by introducing himself or herself and asking the disputants and lawyers for their names. Many mediators like to conduct the mediation using first names to create a familiar and informal atmosphere. The mediator will ask the disputants whether they mind being so addressed and confirm with the mediation participants that they can address the mediator by his or her first name.

Some mediators are uncomfortable conducting a mediation using first names and prefer the formality of surnames. I heard a story about a group of retired judges who were in a mediation training course in the United States and were told that they should allow the disputants and lawyers to address them by using first names. The trainer could see from the judges' faces that there was great discomfort in the room. Eventually, one of the judges said, 'I guess I'll allow them to call me "Your"'.

The mediator will probably then deal with some of the administrative issues, such as confirming that the Agreement to Mediate has been signed, telling everyone where the food and lavatories are, and confirming that the retainer has been received. A sample Agreement to Mediate is at Appendix A.

The mediator will also discuss the time scheduled for the mediation and confirm that everyone is available for it. I used to believe that it was best not to schedule a specific amount of time for a mediation because it should take however long it requires. I now believe that it is very important to set an amount of time for a mediation. Amazing things happen about half an hour before the scheduled end of mediation as both (or all) of the disputants discuss compromises and ideas that they had been reluctant to discuss earlier in the mediation process. I now, therefore, try always to set a time frame for mediations, though I encourage attendees to leave their schedules open for the day in case there is a need to spend more time.

5.3.2   The role of the mediator

The mediator can then describe his or her role. The mediator may clarify that he or she is not a judge and not an arbitrator, and will not make a decision for the disputants. The role of the mediator is to facilitate the negotiation so that the disputants can explore whether there is a solution that is better for both of them than continuing to fight the dispute. The mediator can explain that the role of the disputants in the mediation is to persuade each other, not the mediator. Even if a disputant completely persuades the mediator about the fairness or legal consequence of a particular issue, that will not benefit the disputant if the other disputant is not persuaded. The mediator will leave the mediation completely persuaded, and the disputants will leave without a resolution.

It is important, however, for the mediator to make clear to the disputants that he or she may discuss with them the difficulties in and the persuasiveness of some of their arguments. Even a facilitative mediator will help disputants analyse whether a particular argument will persuade a judge.

5.3.3   Good faith and full disclosure

Should the mediator ask (or even require) the disputants to negotiate in good faith and make full and complete disclosure? Why not? Why would we ever condone negotiating in bad faith? Isn't settlement more likely (especially a fair settlement) where there is full disclosure? Many mediators require the disputants to agree to make full disclosure and negotiate in good faith. I am not one of them.

First, the issue of disclosure. If the disputants were negotiating by themselves, they would not be required to disclose anything that they chose not to disclose. While litigation has disclosure rules, negotiation does not (except, of course, that they cannot perpetrate a fraud). Why should disputants be required to disclose something in a mediation that they would not be required to disclose in a negotiation (if the mediator were not there)?

As for the requirement to negotiate in good faith, what does it mean? If someone claims that an offer is 'as far as I'll go', but then makes a further concession, is that bad faith negotiating? Is it lying? Is it posturing? What is the difference? If a disputant does not disclose a fact that, if known, would have a substantive impact on what a trial judge would do, is that bad faith? The disputant would not have to disclose the fact at a negotiation and it may not come out at trial.

The test that I use is as follows: I believe that disputants in a mediation should be free to disclose what they choose to disclose, and act with the same restrictions (or lack thereof) that they would have in a private negotiation. I believe they should not be forced in mediation to do something that they would rightfully choose not to do in a negotiation.

That is not to say that I, as a mediator, would allow one of the disputants to perpetrate a fraud. I would not. But a disputant is not allowed to perpetrate a fraud in a negotiation or a mediation, so my test is still valid, I believe. I therefore do not require people to negotiate 'in good faith'.

5.3.4   Legal advice

When the mediator is a lawyer, the mediator will have to clarify the role that he or she is playing. The mediator will explain that he or she is acting as a mediator, not as a lawyer, and the disputants should rely on their lawyer for legal advice, not on the mediator. The clarification is important because there are obligations on lawyers (such as the obligation of full disclosure to both clients when the lawyer simultaneously represents two clients) which could inhibit a person's ability to act as a lawyer and an effective mediator simultaneously. Mediators who are lawyers should therefore clearly state that they will not be giving legal advice.

Nor should a mediator who is not a lawyer give legal advice. If a non-lawyer gives legal advice, that may be viewed as the unauthorised practice of law. The non-lawyer should therefore explain to the disputants that he or she is not there to provide legal advice and that nothing that the mediator says during the mediation should be considered legal advice.

If the disputants do not have lawyers, the mediator should advise them that they are free to stop the mediation at any time to seek a lawyer's advice if they feel that would be beneficial.

5.3.5   Confidentiality

A mediation can be a closed mediation, in which case the process is a confidential one, or an open mediation, in which case there is no requirement to keep information confidential. Open mediations occur most commonly in matrimonial disputes where the mediator reports to the judge, giving an opinion with respect to (among other issues) the best interests of the children. Most mediations are closed and therefore confidential.

In a confidential mediation, the participants cannot discuss the content of the mediation with people who are not participating and have not signed the mediation agreement (which contains a confidentiality provision) without the permission of the other disputants. The issues in the mediation may or may not be confidential, and the confidentiality of a mediation refers only to statements made in the mediation, not to the issues in dispute.

As stated earlier, if a disputant must report back to someone else at the disputant's organisation about what has occurred at the mediation, the disputant should disclose the obligation to report and make sure that those present are in agreement about any limits on the reporting.

The confidentiality requirement also applies to the mediator. The Agreement to Mediate will usually provide that the mediator must keep confidential any information disclosed in the mediation. There are usually, however, some exceptions to the mediator's requirement to keep information confidential.

The first is that the mediator can disclose information to third parties if the disputants agree that the mediator should disclose. The disputants may both agree, for example, that the mediator should speak to the press after the mediation and disclose some of the content of an agreement that was reached. The mediator will usually require written consent of both (or all) disputants before disclosing.

The mediator can also disclose information to one of the confidential advisors retained by one of the disputants. If, for example, the accountant for one of the disputants calls the mediator and asks about the structure of a settlement, the mediator can talk about the structure without the other disputant's permission (provided the disputants have agreed that the result of the mediation can be disclosed to the accountant). Many mediators ask the disputants to consent to allow the mediator to disclose information from the mediation, on an anonymous basis, for educational or research purposes. That enables me to include the examples in this book.

Finally, the Agreement to Mediate will usually provide that the mediator can disclose information learned if that information suggests an actual or potential threat to human life or safety, or the commission of a crime in the future. If the information emerges that suggests that someone may be injured or even killed, the mediator can disclose such information to the authorities. Similarly, if the mediator learns that a crime will be committed, the mediator can report that to the authorities. It should be noted that the mediator is not given the authority to report information relating to a past crime that he or she obtains in the context of the mediation.

5.3.6   Without prejudice

Discussions in mediations where litigation has been or could be commenced, like settlement discussions, are without prejudice. Unfortunately, mediation participants often misunderstand the term 'without prejudice'. Some believe that the term implies that nothing that is said in the mediation can be used against the person saying it. That is not exactly true. At the end of mediations, people do not go through machines erasing their memories, causing them to forget information that was provided in the mediation. What is learned in the mediation is learned and the learning cannot be undone.

Others say that without prejudice means that, if something is discussed at the mediation, it cannot be discussed if the case goes to trial (or arbitration). This is also not true. Just because an issue is raised at the mediation does not prevent that issue from being raised again at trial. Any issue that could have otherwise been raised at trial can still be raised at trial.

Without prejudice means that, if the litigants go to trial or to arbitration, they cannot refer to what was said at the mediation to prove a fact. If an admission is made at a mediation, the admission is not admissible at trial because it was said at the mediation. If the fact can be proven some other way, however, the evidence is admissible if it is not inadmissible for other reasons. Witnesses cannot volunteer information about what occurred at the mediation and cannot be asked about their recollection of what was said at the mediation.

Because evidence of what has occurred at mediation is not admissible at trial, the Agreement to Mediate will usually provide that the mediator cannot be called as a witness and the mediator's notes cannot be produced as evidence. Many mediators destroy their notes a number of weeks after the mediation.

Where settlement offers are made at mediation, the content of the offer (or even the fact that the offer was made) cannot be disclosed to the trial judge (before a decision is rendered). If an offer is accepted, however, that acceptance of the offer is binding in the same way that any offer that is accepted is binding.

The basis for the rule that statements made at mediation are not admissible at trial is to encourage full and frank disclosure in settlement discussions without fear that a statement will be relied upon by the other disputant if the matter ends up in court.

I should note that the without prejudice nature of settlement discussions and statements made at mediation may not apply to the discussion at trial about legal costs. After a decision has been rendered at trial, if the trial judge asks for submissions relating to costs, offers made to settle the litigation (including those made in mediation) may be admissible.

5.3.7   Authority

A standard Agreement to Mediate usually states that participants in the mediation should have the authority to settle the dispute. When setting the table, the mediator will usually confirm with the disputants that those with authority are at the table, and that there is no one else who needs to be contacted before an agreement is reached.

It Happened at Mediation

If a mediator forgets to ask the disputants whether they have the authority to settle, it is a mistake that the mediator will only make only once. Let me tell you about my 'once'. I was mediating a dispute where the claimant had sued the defendant company for wrongful dismissal and harassment. The claimant attended with her lawyer, and the company president and two vice-presidents attended with their lawyer. I assumed that everyone in the room had authority and that consequently there was no need to raise the point.

A couple of hours into the mediation, I was in a private meeting (a caucus) with the company representatives who were considering an option that had been raised by the claimant. When the company president said that the option might be workable, I asked him whether he was prepared to make an offer. He said that he was not. When I asked him why, he told me that he was under strict instructions from his board of directors not to make any offers, not to accept any offers, and not to take any offers back to the board recommending their acceptance. He could take back offers for the board to consider, but could not recommend acceptance.

After I got up off the floor, I called the claimant into the room to explain the situation and admitted that I had made a mistake by not asking about authority at the commencement of the mediation. The claimant said that she 'expected nothing less' from this company, and said that she was not surprised at the company's posturing. We decided to adjourn the mediation until the people with authority could attend.

When those with authority are not present, the disputants and mediator must establish what will happen if the disputants present at the mediation agree on a resolution to the dispute. Sometimes those with authority can be reached by telephone and the mediation proceeds with the decision-maker available by telephone to approve any agreement that is reached. This process is not ideal, however, because the decision-maker will not have heard what was said at the mediation, and will not have benefited from what was learned. The decision-maker may not understand the reasons for the give and take that occurred in the mediation. However, it may be impractical for the decision-maker to attend the mediation (for reasons of distance or previous commitments) and he or she may only be able to participate by telephone.

It Happened at Mediation

I was mediating a dispute relating to the interpretation of a lease. The landlord said that the lease allowed it to collect an administrative fee on the council tax that it paid on the tenant's behalf, while the tenant argued that the better interpretation of the lease was that it did not allow the landlord to collect a fee. The landlord was a small company and the company president attending the mediation had full authority. The tenant was a large retail chain and had a junior person attend the mediation. The person in attendance had limited authority, but the decision-maker was available by telephone.

Both disputants were represented by experienced lawyers. Though each side argued that its interpretation was the better one, both realised through the discussion that the issue could be interpreted either way by the court. Those in attendance also agreed that the disputants had an ongoing relationship and it therefore made more sense for them to reach a resolution rather than go to court.

> It appeared that those in attendance were close to reaching a consensus on one avenue for settlement, and the tenant asked to be left alone to call a senior vice-president of the company to discuss the potential settlement. I left the company representative (and lawyer) alone so that they could make the call.
>
> When I returned, they told me that the vice-president (not having been privy to the discussions at the mediation) was adamant that the tenant's case was strong, and was not prepared to accept its lawyer's recommendation to reach a settlement that involved any payment of an administrative fee. The vice-president instructed those present not to call him back, and he did not want to speak to me.
>
> Unfortunately, even though everyone in attendance at the mediation believed that it made sense to settle on the terms that we had discussed, the tenant had no authority to reach a deal on those terms and the mediation ended with no deal.
>
> I learned later that the disputants did settle, but only when the president of the landlord company became personally involved in trying to settle it. Ironically, it settled on terms almost identical to those that were tentatively agreed to at the mediation, but after significant time and legal costs.

Some organisations, such as banks, have a decision-making hierarchy that requires people who do not attend mediations or settlement conferences to approve any agreement that is reached. In such cases, the disputants can agree to make any agreement reached at the mediation subject to approval by the senior person who is not in attendance. Once that person approves the deal, it becomes a binding agreement.

A concern that is sometimes raised about this process, however, is that it is unequal and unfair. One side is asked to commit to what has been proposed at the mediation and the other side (such as the bank) is given time to consider the proposal. Some mediations therefore adjourn if a tentative agreement is reached. During the adjournment, the disputant who did not have authority (such as the bank) can seek authority, and the disputant who had authority at the mediation can consider whether to accept or reject the tentative agreement. When the mediation resumes, both sides will have the authority to agree on the tentative agreement and both can commit together. If either side rejects the deal, there will be no agreement.

What does it mean to have full authority? Few business people at a mediation have unlimited authority. While the participants often state at the mediation that they have full authority to settle, such authority is often limited by instructions from a superior. A common example of limited authority occurs in the context of insurance litigation, where a defendant is an insurance company. The insurance company representative at the mediation will probably have a limit on the amount that the insurance company is prepared to pay to settle the claim.

In such cases, some mediators attempt to determine the limit before the mediation commences to satisfy themselves that the limit is 'reasonable'. One of the dangers of dealing with the issue up front is that it can unnecessarily cause the mediation to terminate on the issue of authority – unnecessarily because the issue may never arise. It forces the mediator to do an assessment of whether the limit is reasonable. It is often not possible for a mediator (or anyone else) to assess the reasonableness of the limit and predict whether a settlement agreed by the disputants will be inside or outside the limit. It would be unfortunate not to conduct the mediation on the basis of lack of authority where the person did in fact have authority to agree to what would have eventually been acceptable to the other side.

Another danger of checking the limit of authority is that, when the mediator learns its extent, that may affect the way the mediator conducts the mediation. The person with limited authority may not want to disclose its extent to the mediator for fear that the mediator will encourage the company to agree to pay at least the amount of the limit.

I therefore attempt to deal with the issue of limited authority, if and when it arises, later in the mediation. At the commencement of the mediation, I confirm with the disputant who has limited authority that someone at the company who has more authority is available by telephone. If it turns out that a telephone call needs to be made, the other disputant (who has no issue about authority) can gain comfort in the knowledge that his or her power of persuasion influenced the other side to seek authority to pay more than the limit.

5.4   GROUND RULES

There are a number of ground rules that a mediator may set at the commencement of the mediation to maximise the likelihood that the process will run smoothly and will result in an agreement.

5.4.1   One person speaks at a time

One ground rule is that one person speaks at a time. This sounds simple, logical and easy to follow, but can become difficult for many disputants to adhere to when they become frustrated at the other side's allegations. The mediator may therefore enforce the ground rule by asking disputants to write their comments down when they think of them so that they can recall them when it's their turn to speak. Enforcing a 'one-person-speaking-at-a-time' ground rule can sometimes, in and of itself, help resolve a conflict.

It Happened at Mediation

A law school classmate of mine told me of his experience in mediation and said that he was disappointed in the mediation process. He told me that he had been acting for a claimant in a personal injury dispute and that, because he and the other lawyer had not been able to settle the dispute, they decided to attempt mediation. The mediator introduced himself, set a few ground rules (such as requiring one person to speak at a time), and then did absolutely nothing except enforce the ground rules. My classmate was disappointed that the mediator did not do more to assist the disputants to settle the dispute.

I told my classmate that I understood his frustration, and I asked him where the matter stood now. He told me that he and the other lawyer had settled the case at the mediation, but that it had nothing to do with the mediator.

There are some mediators who believe that setting a ground rule that requires one person to speak at a time is not helpful, and may even harm the process. These mediators believe that frustration escalates when people have to control their feelings, and that the mediator should allow interruptions and facilitate the communication so that the discussion does not get out of hand. Disputants will vent their feelings more freely and will therefore be more likely to settle.

Other mediators do not set the ground rule initially, but institute it later if they find that the disputants are constantly interrupting and not listening to each other.

While I understand the concerns raised by these mediators, I have found the 'one-person-at-a-time' ground rule to be effective. The difficulty with conducting the mediation without the ground rule is that it is so easy for the mediation to get out of control and, if it does, the mediator does not have a ground rule to fall back on.

However, there are situations where the disputants are more comfortable without a one-person-at-a-time ground rule.

It Happened at Mediation

I was mediating a dispute in New York, trying to help two organisations agree on a process for fundraising and the distribution of funds raised. There were five people in the room. I set the 'one-person-speaking-at-a-time' ground rule and we were not more than five seconds into the mediation before one person interrupted another. I reminded everyone of the ground rule and they agreed to try to abide by it. Ten seconds later, though, someone else interrupted and then everyone started talking at once.

Facetiously, I asked the group whether they preferred to speak one at a time or whether they wanted to interrupt whenever they felt the urge. They looked at me and explained that they much preferred to interrupt and be interrupted, as that was how they communicated best. While I was sceptical of proceeding without the ground rule, I knew that it would not be productive to impose a process on them if that process made them uncomfortable.

There were constant interruptions and arguments throughout the day. At the end of the mediation, however, the disputants were able to work out a solution that was satisfactory for all of them.

I learned a valuable lesson at that mediation: it is more important for the disputants to be comfortable with the mediation process than for me to impose a process that suits me.

5.4.2   No personal attacks

A number of mediators set a ground rule prohibiting personal attacks. After all, how can personal attacks be helpful to the mediation process? The mediator will ask the disputants to focus on solving the problem, not on attacking each other. But what is a personal attack? If a former employee says that she was dismissed from a company because of her race, is that a personal attack or is she just stating her belief? If disputants censor themselves by not stating all of the facts because they fear such facts may be interpreted as personal attacks, is that good?

One difficulty with the 'no-personal-attacks' ground rule is that it sometimes conflicts with the goal of allowing disputants to express themselves freely. There is a fine line between describing facts and personal attacks. One person may feel that he or she is venting emotions, while the other person may feel attacked.

If the ground rule is in place, the mediator will have to determine, in each case, whether the comments made are helping the process move forward or are causing it to digress. The mediator will base that determination, in part, on the impact those comments have on the other disputant.

Some mediators, therefore, do not set the ground rule prohibiting personal attacks. They believe that people should say what is on their minds and should not censor themselves by refraining from what may be perceived as personal attacks. They will usually recommend that the disputants treat each other with respect, but state that there is no rule limiting what disputants can say. Each disputant should present whatever he or she believes is important to help resolve the dispute.

5.4.3   Use of inappropriate language

Some mediators set a ground rule that there be no swearing or inappropriate language in the mediation. They believe that swearing increases the likelihood that the mediation will deteriorate and prevent the disputants from reaching a deal. Others feel that the disputants should use whatever language they feel is appropriate, even if the language makes the mediator uncomfortable. A mediator of construction disputes, for example, who is uncomfortable with swearing, may significantly restrict discussion by setting a ground rule prohibiting foul language.

Even where mediators allow people to speak in any way that is comfortable for them, the mediators will intervene if it becomes apparent that one of the disputants is uncomfortable with the language and one is not. The mediator would then facilitate a discussion to find a ground rule that would allow the mediation to continue so that both disputants could negotiate comfortably.

5.4.4   Caucus rules

The mediator will explain to participants that it is likely that, at some point in the mediation, the disputants will have private meetings, also known as caucuses, with the mediator. The caucus will be discussed in more detail in Chapter 10, 'Selecting the Durable Option'. During caucuses, people may wish to disclose to the mediator confidential information that they do not want the other disputant to know. Most mediators are prepared to hear confidential information, but ask the disputants to make sure that they tell the mediator what information is confidential so that he or she will know what not to disclose to the other side.

Sometimes the entire mediation is conducted in a caucus because, for example, the acrimony is so severe that the disputants do not want to be in the same room with each other. For those mediations, the mediator will have to repeat setting the table in each room, making sure that all disputants understand the process and the ground rules.

5.4.5 Termination of the mediation

The mediator will want to discuss with the disputants how the mediation can end. Mandatory mediations (mediations where a law or contract requires that the mediation take place) usually require the disputants to attend for a minimum period of time. During the minimum time, no disputant may unilaterally terminate the mediation and, even if both disputants agree that the mediation should not continue, they cannot end the mediation without the mediator's consent. At the end of the mandatory period, the mediation becomes voluntary.

For voluntary mediations, either disputant can terminate the mediation by walking out or refusing to participate.

Sometimes people threaten to terminate the mediation as a bargaining tactic. Many mediators, therefore, set a ground rule that if any disputant wants to terminate a voluntary mediation, he or she can do so, but only after having a caucus of five minutes with the mediator. If, at the end of that meeting, the disputant still wants to terminate the mediation, the mediation will be over. This meeting gives the mediator an opportunity to salvage a mediation that may appear to be falling apart.

The mediator will probably also inform the disputants that the mediator may terminate the mediation (though it is rare for a mediator to end a mediation while the disputants still wish to talk). A mediator could decide to end a mediation, for example, where he or she obtains information which suggests that there is a fraud being perpetrated in the mediation.

While it is not for the mediator to assess whether a deal is fair, it is also not for the mediator to participate in a fraud. Mediators will usually let disputants negotiate in the best way they are able, and not impose the mediator's sense of fairness and justice. There are limits, however. If the mediator knows that one side is perpetrating a fraud on the other, the mediator will resign rather than be a party to the fraud. Disputants need to have confidence in the mediator and the mediator's ethics. The issue of when and how a mediator should resign is discussed in Chapter 11, 'Overcoming Obstacles'.

5.5   OUTLINE OF THE PROCESS

Before asking disputants about their perspectives on the dispute, the mediator will probably describe the process that the mediation will follow. The mediator will explain, for example, that the first stage of the mediation will be an opportunity for each disputant to provide his or her perspective on what has happened to lead up to the mediation; the next stage will be for the mediator to ask questions to try to understand what was said; the disputants will then see if they can agree on the issues to be determined; there will then be a session that will allow options to be brainstormed; finally, the disputants will have an opportunity to assess the options and determine whether there is one that is better for both (or all) of them than proceeding with litigation.

5.6   THE TEST FOR DISPUTANTS

The mediator may end the setting the table stage by reminding the disputants of the test they need to apply to decide whether to settle the dispute. Disputants often assume that the test is whether the offer is fair, reasonable, just, appropriate or what a court would do. None of those is the test. The appropriate test is whether the offer is better or worse than proceeding without an agreement. For disputes in the context of litigation, not settling means continuing with the litigation.

5.7   HOW MUCH TIME SHOULD SETTING THE TABLE TAKE?

A mediator must balance two goals in determining the appropriate amount of time required to set the table. If the time is too long, the disputants will become frustrated and bored. They will stop listening, as they will be thinking about what they are going to say rather than what the mediator is explaining. The mediator will need to watch for signs that the disputants are bored and, if they are, the mediator should attempt to speed up the introduction.

The danger of disputants getting bored must be balanced with the need to comfort participants, set ground rules and create a sense of anticipation that will encourage disputants to work towards an agreement. Setting the table is not just for a transmission of information from the mediator to the disputants; it is also an opportunity for the disputants and their lawyers to assess the mediator (and his or her style) and to watch each other to see the reaction to some of the things that the mediator says.

My setting the table stage of the process usually takes five to ten minutes. I have found that is not too long so as to bore participants, and is enough time to get out the necessary information.

5.8   PURELY FACILITATIVE SETTING OF THE TABLE

Some facilitative mediators believe that because the disputants are the ones who must live with any result, and because the disputants will be, by and large, coming up with the result, the disputants should establish the process and set the table. These mediators believe that it is unhelpful and perhaps even inappropriate for the mediator to impose a process.

The theory is that, if the disputants are left to flounder and come up with their own rules for the mediation, they will learn from the process of establishing ground rules and coming up with a structure. They will gain valuable experience in working together to solve a problem (which, in this case, is how to come up with appropriate rules for the mediation).

A purely facilitative mediator may therefore commence the mediation by saying nothing and listening to participants argue. After a few minutes of an unstructured process, the mediator will ask whether the process being used (which usually involves accusations) is working. The disputants will usually respond that the process is clearly not working, and that is why they engaged a mediator. The mediator may then ask what the disputants want to do about the process. The disputants may then ask the mediator to create some ground rules. The mediator will ask the disputants what ground rules they would find helpful and the disputants will attempt to create their own.

This purely facilitative method of setting the table is relatively rare, however, because some disputants will become frustrated with the mediator for not controlling the process and keeping the focus. The process can become cumbersome and time consuming. Disputants are often busy people and want to focus on the problem they are there to resolve rather than on the process of mediation. They believe that they are paying the mediator to manage the process and want the benefit of the mediator's experience to help them work through their issues.

In some situations where there is an ongoing relationship, however, purely facilitative setting the table can be used to help disputants not only solve their dispute, but also practise a process that can help them resolve future conflict.

Tips for Lawyers

- The mediator will usually start the mediation with an introduction in which the mediator will set out the process to be followed and establish ground rules. You should ask questions if any part of the introduction is unclear or is different from what you anticipated. Your client should also feel free to ask questions if any part of the introduction is unclear.

- Watch the reactions of the other disputant and lawyer while the mediator is setting the table. You may get a sense of their demeanour and level of anxiety.

Tips for Mediators

- A mediator needs to make sure he or she has the following items for a mediation: enough chairs, coffee and food, a break-out room for caucuses, telephones in each room, paper and pen, a flipchart, marker and tape.

- While setting the table, the mediator should try to speak in a calming way. The disputants will often be emotional and will be caught up in the facts of the dispute. By speaking calmly, the mediator can sometimes relax the disputants and help them focus on the issues.

- You can begin setting the table by asking whether disputants are comfortable using first names. You can then tell them about the time set for the process, the food arrangements, and the location of lavatories and telephones.

- You can then describe the mediation process, and your role in it, explaining that you are not a judge and you are there to facilitate the discussion. The disputants are there to try to persuade each other, not you.

- You will want to mention that you will not be giving legal advice to the disputants.

- You will need to discuss the degree to which the process is confidential and without prejudice. You may need to explain the concept of without prejudice to the disputants.

- You will also want to remind disputants that they have agreed not to call you as a witness at trial.

- You will want to determine whether the people at the mediation have the authority to settle. If they do not, you will need to establish what will happen if those in attendance reach a tentative agreement.

- You will probably want to set ground rules such as requiring that one person speak at a time. You may also want to set a ground rule that there be no personal attacks or inappropriate use of language, or you may omit some or all of these ground rules, giving disputants the freedom to say what they want.

- You will want to raise the point that caucuses may be useful and that people should then feel free to disclose confidential information to you. They should advise you, however, if any information that is disclosed to you is confidential; otherwise, you will assume that you are free to disclose the information to the other side.

- You will then want to outline the mediation process.

- You may want to end by reminding the disputants that their task is not to find the perfect solution, the fair solution or the just solution; rather, their task is to see if there is a solution that is better for both (or all) of them than continuing with the dispute, because that is what will occur if they do not settle.

- As an alternative to the organised process of setting the table, you may choose to leave it to the disputants to set ground rules and organise the process.

- For most disputes the setting the table phase should last no more than 10 minutes.

CHAPTER 6

STORYTELLING

6.1 GETTING THE FACTS

Once the mediator has set the table, the disputants or their lawyers need to present their perspectives on the dispute. How is this done? Who should present first? Should lawyers or disputants speak? How long should presentations be? What should they talk about? Should they ever tell their stories in a private meeting (caucus) rather than directly to the other side?

Storytelling is an opportunity for disputants to tell their stories to the other side, without interruption, usually for the first time. Disputants can talk about whatever they want, regardless of the relevance to the dispute. There is no issue of 'admissibility of evidence' in the storytelling. The disputants have the opportunity to present their views with no one interrupting, even to ask clarifying questions. Often, their views are also their positions, though sometimes they talk about their underlying interests and the possibilities for settlement.

The storytelling provides participants with an often needed opportunity to express their feelings. The disputants usually attempt to portray how they have been wronged and how they believe they have acted reasonably.

People often express strong emotions during the storytelling. For particularly emotional issues, it is not unusual to have tears, yelling and a lot of frustration. The role of the mediator is not to stifle these emotions, but rather to allow them to come out and be heard in a way that facilitates resolution of the dispute.

6.2 LAWYERS OR THEIR CLIENTS

Who should speak – lawyers, clients or both? Some mediators believe that it is important that the clients speak, as opposed to the lawyers. Some even explicitly state that they want the clients and not the lawyers to speak. They fear that, if only the lawyer speaks, there will be no cathartic venting. These mediators have observed that people often feel better after they have vented their emotions and may be more co-operative in the mediation that follows.

Some lawyers, however, feel that they are there to represent their clients and are being paid to speak, so it is important that they present the story in its best light. They hope to persuade the other side by the strength of the story and they worry that, if their clients present the facts, they may present them in a non-persuasive way. They may also be concerned that their clients are emotional and may be confrontational and aggressive during the storytelling while the lawyer can remain detached and objective.

Also, the disputants may be uncomfortable speaking and may prefer to have the lawyer present the story.

There is no right answer as to whether the lawyer or the client should do the storytelling. I believe that, generally, it is best if both the lawyer and the client participate. Both are essential players in the mediation, and the greater their participation early on, the better. I would not alienate the lawyer by asking only the client to speak, excluding the lawyer. I do not believe it would be appropriate to stop a lawyer from speaking for a client. However, I do see the benefit of the client participating in the storytelling.

I usually recommend that the lawyer present the legal issues and the client present the factual issues and business objectives. The lawyer is, for obvious reasons, the best person to present the legal arguments, and the client usually has the most direct knowledge of the facts and of the business goals that led to the establishment of the relationship that has now deteriorated. The client also has the emotions that need to be expressed (and acknowledged).

While my preference is for both the lawyer and client to speak during the storytelling, I do not require them both to speak and I leave it to them to choose who tells the story. My overriding goal is that everyone be comfortable with the mediation process and participate in a way that makes them feel comfortable.

It Happened at Mediation

Family business disputes are, unfortunately, relatively common. In this case, the father had run a company for many years, and had died relatively unexpectedly. The mother and daughter attempted to run the business but could not agree on an approach or strategic direction. The daughter and one of the staff members therefore left the company and formed a competing company. The mother sued the daughter.

I believed that it was important that the mother and daughter talked directly. They were, after all, mother and daughter. The lawyer for the daughter believed that, because the issue was in litigation, the disputants should only talk about the law relating to breach of fiduciary duty and should avoid talking about any facts not directly relevant to the litigation. He believed that he was familiar with all of the relevant facts and advised his client (the daughter) not to speak in the mediation. She agreed.

I had a caucus with the daughter and her lawyer and attempted to persuade them to have the daughter participate by speaking in the mediation, but the lawyer was adamant and the daughter followed her lawyer's advice. Needless to say, the case did not settle.

I believe that the lawyer made a strategic mistake at the mediation. The problem between the disputants and the issue in litigation are rarely identical and, in order to settle, disputants need to solve the real problem, not just the litigation issues. Particularly where there is an ongoing relationship, disputants need to express what is important to them. My failure was in not persuading the lawyer of my belief.

6.3   HOW MUCH TIME FOR STORYTELLING?

There is no rule governing the appropriate amount of time for storytelling. For a typical wrongful dismissal or breach of contract case, the storytelling will usually take about 10 minutes to half an hour per side. For more complex disputes, it can take as much as 45 minutes per disputant. It is rare for storytelling for one disputant to last more than 45 minutes and, when it does, it usually means that either the person is going into too much detail or is getting repetitive. In either case, the mediator will usually gently ask the person to wind up the storytelling so that the mediation can proceed to the next stage (or to the next person's storytelling).

Some mediators explicitly set a fixed time for storytelling to allow people to plan their presentations. Most mediators, however, do not set time limits and only stop the process when people feel that they have said all that they need to say.

It Happened at Mediation

I was conducting a six-party mediation where the claimant had sued numerous defendants relating to the alleged negligent construction of his house. Insurance companies represented some of the defendants. The mediation was scheduled for only five hours. I realised that if I allowed disputants to speak as long as they wanted during storytelling and if they each took about half an hour, we would be using up more than half of our time and would not have enough time for problem solving. I therefore set a ground rule that storytelling would be limited to 10 minutes per disputant and I enforced the ground rule.

We completed the storytelling, problem-solved and were on the verge of a solution when the claimant said, 'You know, none of this would have happened if the insurance companies would have returned phone calls', to which an insurance company representative replied, 'We did return phone calls; you weren't home'. From there, the disputants started arguing about what had happened in relation to some telephone calls. Emotions began to run high.

I realised that I had not allowed enough time for storytelling and all of the facts that the disputants considered relevant had not been uncovered. Before the disputants could sign an agreement, they needed to discuss the issue of the telephone calls and I had to allow another round of storytelling. After they had an opportunity to vent their feelings, they signed the agreement.

The lesson for me was not to minimise the importance of storytelling and to allow the necessary time for people to talk about what is important to them.

6.4 WHO GOES FIRST?

If the mediation takes place in the context of litigation, it is usually understood that the claimant (and lawyer) will speak first. The mediator will usually suggest that the claimant proceed first, and confirm with the disputants that that is acceptable.

Where the context is other than litigation (say, for example, a dispute among a board of directors), the issue is not so clear. In particularly acrimonious disputes, it may become an issue as to who speaks first in the storytelling. One option is for the mediator to decide who should speak first and make a suggestion to the disputants. The suggestion can be based on the mediator's experience and assessment of the information in the mediation briefs. Another option is for the mediator to ask the disputants to decide who will go first. Usually, they will choose an order without much difficulty; periodically, however, they will argue about who should speak first.

If they do, it is for the mediator to mediate this aspect of the dispute no differently than the mediator would deal with any other issue. The mediator will need to uncover why this issue is important to disputants and try to help them come up with options that can solve the problem. Flipping a coin may be the best solution, or the disputants may agree that one disputant speaks first but has a specific (short) time limit, after which the other person can speak for a short time before the first person resumes.

The mediator will try to resolve the issue quickly. If too much time is spent debating the issue of who speaks first, the disputants may become frustrated and disillusioned with the mediation process.

6.5   GOALS FOR STORYTELLING

The objective in storytelling is to provide each of the disputants with the opportunity to present their views, uninterrupted, and to gain an understanding of the other disputants' perspectives. The disputants can then get a sense of the interests that need to be met and the obstacles that need to be overcome for a settlement to be reached. It also provides an opportunity for the disputants to say things to the other side (whether relevant to the litigation or not) that they want to say.

It Happened at Mediation

Sometimes storytelling can help resolve a dispute in unexpected ways. I was mediating a dispute between a company and one of its former consultants about money allegedly owing under a consultancy agreement. The consultant spoke for an extremely long time in the storytelling phase and said that he believed that it was very important for him to present all of the reasons why he did such a good job for the company (though that was not an issue in the litigation). I let him talk because he felt strongly that he wanted to talk about his work.

In a caucus, the company representative told me that he thought the consultant's story was more fiction than fact, but that it had persuaded him to increase the offer that he had otherwise been prepared to make. When I asked him why, he told me that, after listening to the consultant for the past hour, he was persuaded that litigation would be very time-consuming, expensive and particularly frustrating. He saw great value in avoiding the frustration. The case settled.

6.6   STORYTELLING IN CAUCUS

In some cases, the parties are angry with each other and refuse to be in the same room, even for storytelling. In those situations, the mediator will still need to allow time for storytelling, though it will take place in a caucus. The disputants will want the neutral person (the mediator) to hear about the dispute and they will want to talk about why their proposition for settlement is fair. It may be, after some airing of views, the disputants feel comfortable resuming the mediation in joint session.

It Happened at Mediation

I was mediating a wrongful dismissal case where the employee had worked for a particular company for more than 30 years as a janitor and had been let go because the company downsized. The former employee was so cross with the company that he requested that the entire mediation take place in separate rooms.

During the storytelling, the employee's wife talked about how hard her husband had worked, and the effect that had had on her. I asked her whether she was prepared to talk to the company representatives. She said that she was, and went in the other room to talk to them. When she finished, not only was she in tears, but so were the company representatives. A barrier was broken.

She went back and told her husband what had happened and he agreed to participate with the company representatives in one room. The case settled.

Tips for Lawyers

- In the storytelling, you will have to decide how much you will present and how much your client will present. Often it makes sense for you to present the legal issues and for your client to present the factual issues or business goals. It is almost always helpful for the client to participate in the storytelling, at least to a degree, so that he or she can start to become comfortable with the process and gain some commitment to it. Both you and your client should try to avoid confrontational or antagonistic statements, while still stating the problems and facts.

- This will be the opportunity for your client to see how strongly you can present the case, and to see the other side's case presented. My recommendation is to put forward the summary of the case you would put at trial, and to put it at its strongest. One of the goals of the storytelling is for each disputant to hear the other disputant's case and to have a sense of what would be presented at trial, so as to assess the value of avoiding the risk of going to court.

- It can therefore be helpful to finish the storytelling by expressing optimism about the prospects for settlement, and identifying the reality that litigation can be expensive and time-consuming, so that a deal reached at mediation would be good for both sides. It can also be helpful for both the lawyer and the client to indicate that, while they are prepared to go to trial if necessary, they would prefer to come to an agreed-upon amicable settlement and are open to be persuaded about what is fair.

- There is a tendency for lawyers during the storytelling to try to persuade the mediator rather than trying to persuade the other side. The purpose of the mediation is to try to persuade the other side and the presentations should focus on the other side, not on the mediator. The presentations should not spend a lot of time on the basic facts that everyone knows.

- Storytelling should be concise. Except in unusual circumstances, storytelling should last for about 10 to 15 minutes per disputant.

Tips for Mediators

- It is common to recommend that the claimant go first in storytelling. Ask both sides to decide whether they prefer to have the lawyer present the story, the client, or both. Recommend that the lawyer present the legal issues and the client present the factual issues and business goals.

- During the storytelling, you should take notes of what is said. You may want to draw a vertical line down the page and record what people are saying on the left-hand side of the page. On the right-hand side of the page, you can write any questions or thoughts you have about interests that are being expressed, particularly if the interests are joint. You should try to avoid focusing on solutions at this point.

- As far as possible, you should try to get the disputants to direct their stories to each other rather than to you, though they may feel more comfortable looking at you rather than at each other. Disputants and lawyers will have a tendency to focus their presentations on you in an attempt to persuade you that the other side is being unreasonable and should make compromises. The goal of the disputants, as stated earlier, should be to persuade the other side and not the mediator.

- Sometimes, disputants can repeat themselves. It is a challenge for a mediator to assess when to intervene in these circumstances so as to keep disputants focused, control the time and the process, and not stop the expression of emotions and ideas. My advice is that you allow some repetition but, if there is significant repetition, you should ask the disputant or the lawyer to try to finish in the next couple of minutes.

- Sometimes people start to talk about issues that do not appear to be relevant to the issues in the dispute. I recommend erring on the side of allowing the people in the mediation to say whatever it is they want to say. The tangent may seem irrelevant to you, but the disputants may believe (or know) that it is crucial for them and an important piece of the settlement puzzle. However, if it becomes clear that one side is going off on tangents and the other is becoming frustrated, you may want to interrupt to query the relevance of the topic.

CHAPTER 7

DETERMINING INTERESTS

As we saw earlier, a mediator tries to change a competitive negotiation into an interest-based or principled one. How can a mediator do that? How can he or she uncover the underlying interests? Perhaps most importantly, how can the mediator make sure that the disputants have heard and understood each other?

In storytelling, disputants and their lawyers will usually set out the positions and the legal issues; many mediators will then try to uncover the interests behind the positions. As stated earlier, interests are the wants, needs, desires and goals behind the positions. Positions can only be satisfied one way but interests can be satisfied in many ways.

7.1 GOALS OF IDENTIFYING INTERESTS

Why should a mediator even bother trying to uncover interests? There are a number of reasons.

Uncovering the interests is the key to a productive mediation in that it provides the first clues to settlement options. By encouraging the disputants to focus on interests instead of positions, the mediator forces them to think about what they really want and why. They will then be able to explore the different ways that their interests can be met in the event that the other disputant does not accept their initial position. The positions that are being argued are probably irreconcilable, and a solution can only be reached in negotiation if one or both sides compromise on the positions they are advancing. People are reluctant to make concessions and a settlement is therefore often illusory. Refocusing the discussion on satisfying and balancing interests (rather than having clashing positions) can result in creative and mutually beneficial solutions.

It Happened at Mediation

I was mediating a dispute between two groups that had been feuding for years. One group, a co-operative, represented a number of workers and the other group represented those who hired the workers. There was no employer-employee relationship and the group that represented the workers was not a union. The issue in the mediation, not surprisingly, was the appropriate wage to be paid to the workers. All of the discussions were about money.

When our discussion seemed to be going nowhere, we decided to break into private meetings (caucuses). I talked to the workers' group first.

When I asked the leader of the group why he was so frustrated (which he obviously was), he told me that he was frustrated because the employer group was trying to destroy the workers' co-operative and wanted to negotiate with all of the workers individually. He said that his dream would be for the employers to recognise the right of the co-operative to negotiate on behalf of the workers.

When I talked to the employer group, they said that it would be a nightmare for them to negotiate with all of the workers individually and that they much preferred to negotiate with the co-operative. They did not realise that the workers had the perception that the employer group wanted to destroy it. I had them sign a letter to the co-operative expressing their desire to work with it and officially recognising that the group represented the workers.

The workers' group was thrilled and the balance of the mediation was relatively smooth with significantly more goodwill both ways. The key was uncovering the unstated interest of the co-operative to be recognised as having legitimacy to negotiate for the workers.

It Happened at Mediation

A family moved into its new house and drilled a well to get its water. The water was tested and the family was advised that the water was safe to drink. Members of the family drank the water, bathed in it and used it for the swimming pool. The water had a strange smell, however, so the family arranged to have more detailed tests performed a number of months later, and discovered that the water contained a carcinogen. The family sued the vendor of the property, the real estate agent, the township, the region, and the government. Family members wanted damages for their suffering.

At the mediation, the defendants all agreed that the family was entitled to some money but each defendant believed that someone else should pay the money.

We determined, during the discussion, that the family's overriding interest was getting clean, drinkable water. The family wanted money from the defendants to fund the cost of getting fresh water to the house.

The defendants found it easier to satisfy that interest than to come up with an acceptable amount of money. The vendor of the property had a nearby property and gave some of his land for a well; the government agreed to test the water regularly; the other defendants agreed to build the well (which they could do relatively inexpensively because of contracts they had with various suppliers) and arrange for the construction of a pipeline to get water to the family (which their staff could do relatively easily).

The family's interests were met. They had drinkable water. The defendants, likewise, met their interests of getting drinkable water and minimising the cost of settling the litigation.

A second goal in uncovering interests is to help the mediator understand what is important in the mediation. Some people are sceptical of mediation and some fear that the mediator is only trying to 'get a solution', even if it is at the expense of one of the disputants. By asking questions and uncovering interests, mediators show that they are genuinely trying to understand the issues and the disputants' perspectives and needs.

A third goal in uncovering interests is to help the disputants understand each other. People in a dispute are often so focused on positions and justifications that they do not listen effectively. By asking questions, clarifying and uncovering underlying interests, the mediator can reframe and retell the story, giving others at the mediation an opportunity to hear and understand.

It may take some time and effort to uncover the true interests. People may be reluctant to talk about what they really want, thinking it is irrelevant or that it provides information that may help the other disputant if the case goes to trial.

A fourth goal in identifying interests is to change the focus of the discussion from the past to the future. Disputants in mediation are often focused on the past, on proving what happened, and that they were morally, ethically and legally in the right. The mediation focuses on the future, recognising different perspectives about the past. Once the interests are uncovered, the focus of the mediation can be on how those interests can be met, rather than on proving whose version of the facts is the right one.

7.2   FACILITATING COMMUNICATION

Determining interests involves more than simply asking questions. At this stage of the mediation, many mediators will help the disputants interact with each other so as to ensure that everyone feels heard and that presentations are understood. To do this, the mediator facilitates communication between (or among) the disputants.

The first part of facilitating communication is for the mediator to interact with each of the disputants, showing them that their ideas have been heard and understood. This is achieved through interactive listening.

7.2.1   Interactive listening

Listening involves more than passive listening. Interacting while listening can help clarify misunderstandings, help the speaker feel heard, and create an atmosphere of respect and understanding. Many people focus on their responses while they listen, rather than focusing on the listening itself. When this happens, speakers may not feel heard or understood. Interactive listening forces the listener to focus on what the speaker is saying, rather than on the response, and helps improve communication. Its goal is to make people feel heard. If they do feel heard, they may not feel the need to repeat and argue as much as they otherwise would. There are six techniques of interactive listening that a mediator may use.[1]

Perhaps the most obvious form of interactive listening is paraphrasing. Paraphrasing is taking what a person has said and restating it in the paraphraser's own words. The restatement is not meant to show the speaker why his or her idea is wrong, unfair or ridiculous, it is meant to show the speaker that his or her ideas are understood. Paraphrasing may begin with, 'if I understand you correctly, you seem to be saying . . .', and may end with, 'have I understood you correctly?' Accurate paraphrasing will result in the other person agreeing that you have understood what was said.

The second technique in interactive listening is to ask clarifying questions. Clarifying questions are not ones that challenge the speaker and the speaker's ideas, but rather seek to clarify a point that may not be completely clear.

---

1   I would like to thank Elinor Whitmore for her original ideas on interactive listening that contributed significantly to the content of this section.

The third form of interactive listening is using open body language. A speaker who is listening has open body language (for example, the person does not usually have his or her arms crossed, is leaning forward, is making eye contact and nods at appropriate points). I should say something about nodding before I go on. Nodding can indicate one of two things: either the nodder hears what is being said; or the nodder agrees with what is being said. A person must be careful if nodding to indicate listening (especially when the person does not agree with what is being said), because the same nod could be interpreted by the other person as an indication of agreement with what is being presented.

Observing others' body language is a form of listening. If people look away during storytelling, for example, they send the message that they are not listening and are not interested. If, on the other hand, they look attentive, take notes and smile (if appropriate), they show that they are listening and are interested.

The fourth technique of interactive listening is using 'prompters'. Prompters are words or sounds that signal the speaker to continue. 'Go on' and 'I see' are examples of prompters. Prompters let the speaker know that the listener is listening and wants the speaker to continue.

A fifth form of interactive listening is acknowledging emotions. People express not only words when they speak, but also emotions. Effective interactive listening therefore involves not only paraphrasing the words that have been said, but also paraphrasing the emotions that have been expressed. For example, a person in storytelling may express anger, shame, frustration or may be otherwise upset. A good interactive listener will recognise the emotions and tell the other person that the emotion has been heard.

Finally, a good interactive listener attempts to discover the underlying values of the speaker, though the speaker may not expressly state those values. When people tell their story about a dispute, they usually describe the situation in such a way that they are presented as good people while other disputants are presented as bad people. When disputants speak of the evils that others have perpetrated, they send a message of their values concerning what they believe is and is not acceptable behaviour. The underlying value is the societal norm that the speaker suggests has been broken. For example, a person may say that a neighbour is constantly agreeing to repair the fence but never actually gets around to repairing it. The underlying value could be that people should honour their promises or people should follow through on what they say they will do.

It Happened at Mediation

A woman and her daughter were walking along a street and were hit by a falling tree. They sued the owner of the property alleging that the owner should have been more careful in making sure that the tree did not fall. The evidence was that the owner had known that the tree might fall. Unfortunately, the tree fell on the woman and her daughter before the owner had a chance to remove it.

The woman told the story of how she was pinned by the tree and felt helpless when her daughter, in a frightened voice, called to her mother for help. The daughter had been traumatised because the mother could not comfort her.

After the storytelling, I spent a lot of time interactively listening to try to uncover the interests. The injured mother and daughter needed to be heard. They also needed the owner of the property to acknowledge that he had made a mistake by failing to remove the tree (an admission he had not previously made for fear the admission would hurt him in the litigation). Once it became clear that the mother and daughter had an interest in their suffering being acknowledged, we began to look for ways to satisfy that interest (perhaps in addition to the payment of money).

Eventually, the owner of the property agreed to give the young girl a letter apologising for the accident, saying how sorry he felt that she had been hurt (and had missed her tennis tournament) and hoping that she had made a full recovery. The financial issues were then relatively easy to resolve. The key interest that needed to be met was the need for an apology, and it was the interactive listening that brought out the interest.

For interactive listening to achieve its goals, it is not essential that the listener accurately determines and portrays emotions and underlying interests: what is important is that the listener genuinely tries to understand what is being said. If the listener is wrong, the speaker will provide the appropriate correction.

7.2.2 Direct communication between disputants

Another aspect of facilitating communication in mediation is helping the disputants communicate with each other directly. People hearing the story may not fully understand it and may need clarification of some of the issues raised. They may need to ask each other clarifying questions.

One of the goals of having people speak directly to each other is that they begin the process of communicating. Often, disputants are so angry that they do not talk to each other.

There is a danger in allowing disputants and lawyers to ask questions. The lawyers may try to cross-examine the other disputant to elicit information that could create a strategic advantage at trial. The mediator will need to control the types of questions that are being asked to prevent the mediation from becoming a discovery. That being said, a goal of mediation is for people to speak and listen, and direct communication can have positive and unexpected consequences, regardless of the motive for the communication. I presented earlier the example of the mediation where the insurance company representative told me that he was there only to obtain information to help the insurance company at trial, and to put forward a persuasive case to the claimant. As you will recall, the case settled as a result of the communication, notwithstanding the insurance company's stated intention not to settle.

7.2.3   Role reversal

In addition to having people ask questions of each other, some mediators ask each side to participate in a role reversal to express, in their own words, what they have heard the other person say about a controversial issue.

It Happened at Mediation

I was mediating a dispute among six members of a board of directors of a consulting firm where the issues related to disagreement about the strategic direction of the firm. It became clear early on that there was not a lot of listening among the board members and the communication difficulties exacerbated the problems relating to finding a strategic direction. I decided to initiate a form of role reversal, but with six people. People, in turn, had to present the views of the person next to them, but speak in the first person. Each person had to say how the other person approached his or her work, what the person's philosophy was about the firm, and what the person's goal was for the firm's strategic direction.

The interesting part of the exercise was that people learned that they understood each other a lot better than they had thought, but they had never articulated the understanding. After the exercise, people felt more comfortable discussing strategic direction and coming up with a business plan.

7.3   INTERESTS ON A FLIPCHART

When the process of determining interests, interactive listening and facilitating communication is complete, the mediator may set out some of the ideas on a flipchart. Many mediators use flipcharts to focus disputants on the positive, to keep them looking for solutions and to make sure that everyone agrees with what has been said.

After interests have been uncovered, it can be helpful for a mediator to set out joint interests to show the disputants that they do not disagree about everything and, in fact, have a number of interests in common. I often start with the heading, 'Everyone Agrees', and list the joint interests that have been established. Of course, the list varies depending on what was said during the storytelling and in answer to questions. Joint interests might include, for example, that everyone wants to resolve the issue without litigation, everyone wants to be fair and everyone is concerned about their reputations and wants to leave with them intact.

Some mediators also set out the interests that are opposed. I do not set these out on a flipchart because I prefer to focus on the positive, particularly on the joint interests. That does not mean that I ignore the opposed interests; in fact, I keep a list of those interests on a sheet of paper. I simply find that mediation is more productive if the opposed interests are not set out on the flipchart.

Tips for Lawyers

- One of your challenges in mediation is to determine how your client's interests and the other client's interests can be met. Your task will be easier if you establish the other side's true interests and goals. While the mediator will ask questions to reveal interests, you should be prepared to ask questions as well. The goal of the questions should not be to trap the other person or show them how their presentations are illogical; that is the goal at trial. The goal when asking questions in mediation is to find out why the other disputants are taking the position that they are, and how they will be better off if their position is accepted.

- If the other side asks factual questions of your client, you should not object (as you may on discovery or at trial) to questions that are irrelevant; rather, you should only stop your client from answering questions where the answer would be embarrassing, where the answer may create discomfort for your client or where the question would require your client to make an admission of a fact that you would prefer the other side not have.

Tips for Mediators

- When trying to establish underlying interests, ask 'why' and 'why not'. The goal of asking why is not to learn a justification for the position, but rather to learn the purpose for which the position is being asserted. In other words, you are trying to learn how the person will be better off if the position the person is articulating is accepted at the end of the day. The answer to that question will provide clues to the true underlying interests. You may also ask the disputants why the solution proposed by the other disputant does not satisfy them. Other questions that may reveal interests include asking about what the person sees himself or herself doing in five years, or asking what the disputants' goals were when they first got together.

- When the disputants are all together (in joint session), do not ask questions that you think they or their lawyers may be reluctant to answer, even if you think the answer will be helpful to the mediation process. If you put disputants or lawyers in an uncomfortable position, they will not appreciate it and will be less likely to work with you to find a settlement. You should ask any difficult questions that you may have in caucus. The answers, if they are not confidential, can always be shared later.

- If you find that there are a number of joint interests (as there usually are), you may want to do a list on a flipchart with the heading, 'Everyone Agrees', and list the joint interests. Disputants often lose sight of the fact that there is a lot they have in common and a lot they agree on. A chart of their joint interests can remind them of this and the benefits of working together to resolve their conflict.

- As part of establishing interests, you will often choose to show each disputant that you have heard them by interactively listening to their stories. The listening usually takes the form of paraphrasing the story, asking clarifying questions, using open body language, using prompters, acknowledging emotions and identifying underlying values.

- People in mediation will often want to talk to each other, and you will need to facilitate that discussion. If the questioning turns aggressive, or if one of the lawyers starts objecting to questions, you may want to curtail the process.

- If appropriate (and if the disputants are willing), you may ask disputants to engage in a role reversal exercise.

CHAPTER 8

ISSUES

How should the issues in mediation be drafted? Who should draft them? Are interests and issues the same thing? How should issues be framed to maximise the likelihood that they will lead to settlement?

The issues are the questions that need to be answered in order for the dispute to be resolved. After the interests have been established, the next stage in the mediation is to agree on the issue or issues that need to be resolved.

8.1   ISSUES VERSUS INTERESTS

There is a lot of confusion about the difference between issues and interests. The confusion arises, I think, for two reasons. First, people use the term issues when they mean interests. For example, people say, 'Sam's issues are ...' when they mean to describe his interests. The second reason is that issues are often framed using interests.

Interests are a person's wants, needs, desires and goals. They are the things that a person wants to achieve, that will satisfy the person or make the person happy. Issues are questions that disputants seek to resolve. Once the issues are resolved, the dispute will be over. One of the goals in resolving the issues is to resolve them in a way that meets the disputants' interests.

8.2   HOW TO FRAME ISSUES

Most people frame issues so that they can be answered by a yes or a no. Issues begin, 'Has Company A complied with ... ?' or 'Is Jane responsible for ... ?' Mediators try to frame issues as problems that need to be solved, and problems can rarely be solved with a yes or a no. Mediators therefore frame issues starting with phrases such as, 'How can we ... ?' The balance of the issue statement is a summary of the interests that must be met in order for the case to settle. In other words, the challenge is to find a way that the competing interests can be met and that is how the issue is framed.

For example, in a dispute between two companies about whether a supplier had supplied the appropriate goods, the disputants might say that the issues were: were the goods that were contracted for actually supplied? Was there a breach of contract? What, if any, are the damages? Has the claimant mitigated its damages? This list of questions replicates the legal and factual issues that would have to be determined at trial. The issues have not been framed to reflect the disputants' interests, nor have they been framed in a way that would encourage disputants to think of creative options for settlement.

If the issue were framed as a problem, it might be: 'How can we make sure that the supplier is fairly compensated for what was supplied, and make sure that the purchaser receives material to allow it to complete its manufacturing process?' Here, the issue has been framed to reflect the disputants' underlying interests, which must be met in order for the dispute to be resolved. Beginning the question with 'How can we ... ?' encourages the disputants to try to identify as many different ways of answering the issue as possible. Obviously, the framing of the issue will vary depending on the facts of the dispute and the interests that have been uncovered.

There may be only one issue in the mediation or there may be many. I usually try to reduce what has been said to one issue, if possible, or to a maximum of three issues. However, I have had cases where the interests could not be expressed in three issues and there were numerous issues.

It Happened at Mediation

I was mediating an estate dispute between the executors of an estate and the former caregiver of the deceased. The deceased had no family and her will specified that her estate was to go to the executors who were her friends. Her caregiver sued, arguing that the deceased had promised him that she (the deceased) would give him (the caregiver) her house rather than pay for the care. There was no mention in the will of the agreement.

The disputants could not agree on the facts. The caregiver insisted that the deceased had promised him the house, and the executors insisted that they would have known if the deceased had made that promise and that there must have been no such promise made.

After setting the table, storytelling and the uncovering of interests (including interactive listening and facilitating communication), I told the disputants that, of course, I did not know whether a promise was made. I told them that, similarly, a judge would not know whether the promise had been made. The issue in litigation would be whether the promise was made and whether it was enforceable at law. In court, the judge would have to decide the legal issue.

In mediation, however, the issue was different. Based on what the disputants had said in the storytelling, it seemed that we did not have to decide whether a promise was made in order to settle the litigation and the disputants could continue to believe that a promise was (or was not) made even after a settlement was reached.

There were some joint interests. Each disputant wanted to do what the deceased had wanted, and each disputant had an interest in preserving her memory. We therefore framed the issue as: 'How can we distribute the estate in a way that is fair, that respects the wishes of the deceased, and that preserves her memory?'

Once the issue was framed in this way, one of the lawyers suggested that one option was to take money from the estate and create a memorial for the deceased. Discussion of that option created goodwill and the disputants eventually agreed on an amount to be paid to the caregiver and an amount to be allocated to a memorial.

8.3   WHO SHOULD DRAFT THE ISSUES?

Some people believe that it is best for the disputants to draft the issues since they are closer to the problem and have the information to allow them to draft the issues appropriately. Also, they are the ones who have to solve the problem and it may not be helpful for them to solve a problem that someone else has drafted. The mediator may not get the issue right.

Others believe that the mediator should draft the issue to make sure it is worded in a neutral, problem-solving way. I agree that it is better for the mediator to attempt to draft the issue, and to confirm with the disputants that the mediator has drafted the issue so as to reflect their interests. The mediator can frame this neutrally, so as not to favour one disputant over another. Also, mediators can avoid drafting issues that can only be answered by a yes or a no, drafting them instead as problems that can be solved.

It is not essential for the mediator to glean accurately the perfect issues from what disputants and their lawyers have said; what is important is that the mediator tries to draft the issues. If the mediator gets the issue wrong, the disputants will let the mediator know and the issue statement can be revised. The mediator will still be able to take the revisions that the disputants recommend and make them neutral and focused on problem solving.

When the disputants correct what the mediator has drafted, the mediator may gain new insights into the disputants' interests. The disputants may correct the mediator's drafting of the issue and make suggested amendments that better reflect their interests.

Once the disputants agree on the issue, the mediator will usually list it on a flipchart so that the disputants can see the problem that needs to be solved.

Tip for Lawyers

- When framing issues for mediation, try to frame them in such a way that they cannot be answered by a yes or a no. If they are framed as yes and no questions, it is likely that one disputant will believe that the answer is yes and the other will believe that the answer is no. Ideally, issues should be framed as problems to be solved. Remain open to the issue being framed differently from how it might be framed if the case were to proceed to litigation.

Tips for Mediators

- You may need to be the one framing issues. When doing so, try to frame the issues as problems that need to be solved. One way to do this is to begin with, 'How can we … ?', and fill in the blank with the disputants' interests. Check with the disputants to see if you have accurately reflected their interests.
- Once there is agreement on the issues, post them on the wall so that they are visible throughout the mediation.
- If you are stuck and cannot discern the interests in order to frame the issue, one suggestion is to ask, 'What possible resolutions are there to this dispute that would keep you out of court?' While this framing of the issue is not ideal and is necessarily broad, it may focus disputants on problem solving and help them come up with a workable solution.

CHAPTER 9

BRAINSTORMING OPTIONS

9.1   FINDING CREATIVE SOLUTIONS

How do we move from the issues to possible solutions? Brainstorm options. But who should participate in the brainstorming? Should the mediator brainstorm? How can the mediator encourage creative brainstorming? Should the brainstorming occur with the disputants together or in separate rooms?

Once the issues have been drafted and agreed to, the disputants will start to focus on how the problem can be solved. Commonly in mediation, the disputants will start this process by brainstorming options. Basically, for brainstorming, the disputants try to think of all of the possible solutions to the issues, whether the solutions are ones that they themselves would be prepared to accept or not. Participants, including lawyers, are encouraged to think of good options, bad options and even crazy, ridiculous options. It is amazing how often crazy, ridiculous options can lead to workable, viable options.

While options are being generated, the mediator is usually writing them on a flipchart.

It Happened at Mediation

I was mediating a fee dispute between a lawyer and a former client. The original litigation was a divorce proceeding and the lawyer had represented the wife. The former client believed the bill was unreasonable and the lawyer wanted the bill paid in full.

In the brainstorming process, the lawyer decided to get very creative and said that one option was for the former client to do some work for the lawyer. The lawyer did not believe that this was a feasible option, but was attempting to brainstorm creative solutions. When we began discussing the options, the former client said that the option was unworkable since the travel to and from the lawyer's office would not be possible. It turned out, however, that the former client was a very fast typist. It also emerged that the lawyer was writing a book and did not have enough secretarial assistance to type the book. The disputants eventually agreed that the lawyer would send dictation tapes to the former client who would type what was on the tapes. The disputants agreed on an hourly rate (that was perhaps a bit higher than what was being paid in the office) and the client agreed to pay a percentage of the bill in cash while paying for the balance with her typing.

9.2   TWO GROUND RULES

There are two standard rules for brainstorming that are explained at the commencement of the brainstorming process. It is the mediator's job to establish and enforce the ground rules. The first rule is that there is no commitment to any of the options that are brainstormed. Options are not offers, they are options, and people should feel free to brainstorm without fear that they have committed. Commitment comes at the end of the process, after all of the options have been brainstormed.

The second ground rule is that there be no criticism of options while they are being generated. The brainstorming process is designed to focus on creativity, not on analysis. The analysis of the practicality of options can come later.

It Happened at Mediation

I was mediating a dispute between a manufacturer of office equipment and a group of former employees who had quit and formed a competing company. The manufacturer was suing the former employees for breach of fiduciary duty, claiming that the former employees had taken with them confidential information such as customer lists and pricing. The former employees were counter-claiming against the manufacturer, alleging that people who still worked at the manufacturer were slandering the former employees by suggesting that the former employees were thieves.

We were brainstorming options and I was encouraging the disputants to think of crazy, ridiculous options. One such option generated by the employer (manufacturer) was that the employees could come back to work for the manufacturer. In fact, both sides knew that this was unworkable. There was too much bad blood and it was not a feasible option. It was generated, however, in the spirit of creating crazy options. The employer seemed to regret generating the option and wanted to retract it, and the employees wanted to criticise the option. Both sides knew the ground rules, however, and proceeded without criticise the option until the brainstorming process had concluded.

When we began analysing the options, the former employees suggested that the option be removed from the list, because they would never return to the former employer. The employer responded that that was the first intellligent thing that the employees had said all day. I then asked whether there was any possible good that could flow from that option (not to suggest that it was a good option). The employees said no, and the employer said no. As I was about to move on, the employer said that there could be a small benefit. The employer explained that the former employees had penetrated a new market that the employer had not been able to penetrate and, if the employees returned, perhaps the employer could penetrate the new market. The president quickly added that it would not be worth taking the employees back, however, to get into the new market. The former employees said that if they had to find a benefit to returning to work for the employer, it would be that they would be able to learn more about the new equipment that the employer was now manufacturing, so that they could have this information when they left a second time to form their own company, a scenario they believed was inevitable.

There were obviously some communication and relationship issues to deal with but, after that, the disputants reached a settlement in which the former employees agreed to purchase a minimum amount of equipment, over a five-year period, from the employer. They were allowed to purchase some of the new equipment, and they had to sell 20% of the equipment into the new market that they had penetrated. This was not the crazy solution that had been brainstormed (the former employees returning to work for the employer/manufacturer), but it was an option that came from an exploration of the crazy, ridiculous option.

9.3   COMING UP WITH OPTIONS

It is often difficult for disputants and lawyers to come up with creative options or 'expand the pie'. The first options that are usually brainstormed are the options that each disputant proposes as the fairest way to settle the dispute. Known settlement offers are also presented early in the brainstorming.

In the search for creative options, it can be helpful to refer back to the interests that have been generated. Since disputants are far more likely to accept options that satisfy their interests, it can be helpful to consider interests when brainstorming options.

In order to come up with creative options, disputants and lawyers are more productive if they set aside in their minds the fact that there is a dispute and try to think of what might be achieved if the disputants were starting with a clean slate. They come up with creative options when they assume that the issue is a joint problem that needs to be solved, rather than a battle between two disputants.

That is not to say that everyone should ignore issues of trust and should ignore history; options do not have to be realistically viable. It is always possible (and easy) to eliminate an option at the end of the brainstorming process. It is difficult, however, to come up with the creative options.

I have mentioned previously the benefits to disputants and their lawyers in adopting behaviour that they want others to follow. Brainstorming creates an opportunity to set the tone. People want others to be creative, to come up with options that they do not necessarily agree with at the outset, and to consider the other side's concerns, but these same people are often reluctant to come up with options that they themselves would not be prepared to accept. If we want others to be creative and open-minded, we must be prepared to be creative and open-minded ourselves.

It Happened at Mediation

A couple bought a house in the country and learned, to their chagrin, that the entire property flooded when there was a heavy rain. The purchaser sued the vendor, the council and the city. During the mediation, the disputants first brainstormed the obvious option that the defendants pay money to the purchaser as compensation. The purchaser then said, 'Aren't there any options that will stop my land from flooding?' The disputants then got creative. The vendor, who had a farm, agreed to provide landfill so that the land would be raised to a level where it would not flood. The council provided the topsoil for the land and the city agreed to install a drainage system. The disputants solved the problem in a way that a court never could have.

9.4   WHO SHOULD PARTICIPATE IN BRAINSTORMING?

Disputants and their lawyers should participate in the brainstorming process. The more ideas that are presented, the greater the likelihood that a viable option will emerge from the brainstorming process. If there are experts participating in the mediation, they can also participate in the brainstorming.

It Happened at Mediation

I was mediating a dispute between a bank and a small business. The bank was suing the business for non-payment of interest and principal owing on a bank loan. The business could not afford to pay even the interest on the loan and the bank was about to foreclose. The disputants decided to try mediation. The business owner brought with him his accountant, whom he said could be helpful in the process. The bank representative had reservations about the accountant's attendance because he did not have his own accountant, but finally consented to the accountant's attendance.

During the brainstorming process, the accountant proposed that he might be able to come up with a way that the loan could be restructured to everyone's satisfaction. He came up with a plan for repayment that resulted in the bank getting significantly more than it would have in a foreclosure and gave the business owner the time to recover from his cash flow crisis. He also proposed that the business owner (his client) provide additional security to satisfy the bank (an issue that he had discussed with the business owner in a private meeting (caucus)).

The most creative person in this mediation was neither a disputant nor a lawyer; it was the person who had almost been excluded from the mediation for fear he would be disruptive, irrelevant and unhelpful.

There are two schools of thought on whether the mediator should participate in the brainstorming session. Some mediators believe that it is the disputants who must live with the solution, and they should be the ones coming up with ideas. These mediators argue that the disputants may believe that an option brainstormed by the mediator is the mediator's idea of a fair or just solution and disputants may feel that the mediator is taking sides. People who believe that the mediator should not participate in the brainstorming also express concern that disputants may place undue emphasis on the option or options generated by the mediator.

On the other hand, the mediation process can be enhanced if mediators participate in the brainstorming process. People hire particular mediators because of their insights, experience and expertise, and look to those mediators to contribute ideas and creative solutions.

I freely participate in the brainstorming process when I mediate, believing that if I think of ideas, I should not keep those ideas to myself. At the same time, I am careful not to suggest that my idea is the best or even a viable option. Also, when I present options that I believe may be perceived as favouring one side, I also try to present options that could be perceived as favouring the other side.

9.5   BRAINSTORMING IN JOINT SESSIONS OR CAUCUS?

Is brainstorming best when disputants are together or when they are in caucus? When brainstorming occurs in joint session there can be some advantages that cannot be achieved by brainstorming in caucus. First, the disputants can build on the options generated by each other and come up with interesting and creative options that may not have been generated in private. Secondly, for mediations in which the disputants have an ongoing relationship, brainstorming can give them a process that they can perhaps use to resolve future disputes. They can learn to work together to solve problems in a non-confrontational way.

There are obstacles, however, to brainstorming in joint session and some mediators prefer the brainstorming to occur in caucus. One of the difficulties with joint session brainstorming is that disputants may be reticent to come up with options in front of the other person for fear the other person will seize the option and insist on it. Notwithstanding the ground rule that options are not offers, participants may fear that they will come up with an option that the other side had not considered, and that the other side will focus on that option and insist on its acceptance. They fear that that focus may prevent the other side from considering options that the other side otherwise may have considered.

Another difficulty is that disputants have a tendency in joint session only to brainstorm options that are in their favour, trying to argue in the brainstorming session that the only fair option is one that is good for them. In caucus, they may be more likely to come up with creative options that are not as favourable to them.

A further difficulty with brainstorming in joint session is that disputants may not brainstorm options that would cause them to disclose confidential information. It may be that there is a viable option but a disputant is unwilling to name it because identifying the option will mean the disputant will need to disclose information that he or she does not want to disclose to the other side.

Because there are benefits to brainstorming in joint session, and yet not all options are generated there, many mediators will start the brainstorming process in joint session to see what options can be generated and then move to a caucus where the disputants can talk about the options that they were afraid to discuss in joint session.

It Happened at Mediation

I was mediating a shareholder dispute between the two shareholders of a small company. It became clear during the discussion that both shareholders believed that it would be best for one of the two to purchase the shares from the other, but it was not clear who should sell and who should buy, and it was certainly not clear what the price should be. Both shareholders wanted to purchase the other's shares. We brainstormed in joint session and were unable to come up with an option that made sense for both shareholders, so we broke into caucus.

In the caucuses, each shareholder told me, in confidence, that he wanted to purchase the other shareholder's shares. The only issue would be the price. The lawyer for one side suggested an auction for the shares with the higher bidder purchasing the shares from the other shareholder. The other side thought this was an excellent option, turned it into an offer, and the offer was gladly accepted. My job then changed from mediator to auctioneer.

Tips for Lawyers

- During the brainstorming process, try to be creative and, most importantly, try to make your client be creative. Try to think not only of the obvious, known options, but also those options that you or the other side may not have explored completely. Think about the interests that your client has expressed and try to come up with options that satisfy them.

- Do not be afraid to come up with options that your client would not accept. If you show that you are willing to do this, the other side may be more likely to come up with options that they would not be prepared to accept, and the discussion of these can lead to a good result for your client. You may want to talk to your client before the mediation about the value of brainstorming and the ground rules so that your client will not be surprised if you generate an unusual or creative option. However, you will not want to present an option that will make your client uncomfortable or will cause your client to disclose confidential information.

- If you are unsure about whether you should present an option in front of the other side, you may choose to save that option and discuss it with the mediator in caucus. The disadvantage is that you will not be able to gauge the other side's reaction and you will lose the benefit of the ensuing discussion about the option. The advantage is that you can talk about it with your client and the mediator in confidence.

Tips for Mediators

- Brainstorming options should have two ground rules: first, there should be no commitment to options that are generated (they are not offers); and secondly, there should be no criticism of options while they are being generated. It will be your job to enforce the ground rules.

- Some people will be reluctant to participate in the brainstorming process. You may need to introduce the brainstorming by limiting the amount of time that you will spend on it (sometimes to as little as five minutes) and explaining that you recognise that the process may not be fruitful (as there may be no good creative options).

- If you want to participate in the brainstorming session, there are a couple of things you can do to prevent disputants from thinking that the option you generate is your view of the ideal solution. First, try to present options that have emerged from what participants have said, and explain how you have come up with the option. You may say, 'Since person A said this, and person B said that, it seems that you are both saying that one option is . . .'.

- Another idea is that, when you brainstorm options, be sure to brainstorm a number of them, including those that you know will be unacceptable to each disputant. That way, the disputants will understand that you are participating in a process where everyone is generating not only good options, but also unworkable options.

- In order to encourage participants to brainstorm ridiculous options, you may want to recommend to them that they try first to come up with options that they would not be prepared to accept. Later they can come up with options they would be prepared to accept.

- If the disputants and their lawyers are reluctant to brainstorm, you may choose to use silence as a technique to encourage brainstorming. People often abhor a vacuum and, when there is a vacuum of sound, they tend to want to fill it.

- Another technique is to use analogies and hypotheticals. The people involved in the dispute may not be able to see clearly their own issues because they may be so close to the problem. If you can suggest an analogy and ask for options relating to the analogy, they may come up with ideas that they may not be able to think of for their own situation. You may choose to tell them about your experiences with creative solutions resolving similar disputes.

- You may choose to brainstorm in joint session first, followed by brainstorming in caucus.

CHAPTER 10

SELECTING THE DURABLE OPTION

Perhaps the biggest challenge in mediation is selecting from among the options generated and choosing one that everyone believes is better than their respective Best Alternative to a Negotiated Agreement (BATNA). The option that is selected must be realistic, implementable, durable and one that allows everyone to save face (at least to the degree necessary for them). How should the disputants select the right option? When there are factual disputes, how can the mediator and disputants determine what actually occurred? If they cannot, how can the case settle? If the disputants do not have enough information to make a decision about settlement, what should they do? Who should make the first offer? Should offers be made directly to the other side or should the mediator be the spokesperson? How do disputants know when the offer and counter-offer process is nearing an end? When (if ever) should they make a 'final offer'? Should disputants consider offers with the mediator in the room or out of the room? In the end, how should disputants decide whether to accept the best offer they can attain or walk out of the mediation?

10.1   FOCUS ON THE FUTURE

In mediation, it is common for disputants to focus on the past and try to determine who was right, who was wrong, who was acting fairly, and who acted inappropriately. That approach will usually lead to both sides believing that they are in the right and that the other side should accede to what they believe are reasonable demands.

In selecting the best option, the challenge for the disputants is to focus on the future, not the past. Rather than arguing about who is right and who is wrong (an argument that can rarely be resolved), the disputants should focus on what they need to do to resolve the dispute. They do not have to agree with the other person's view of who is right, but they can acknowledge that they understand how the other person could see the situation differently than they do, and then agree on a future course of action.

10.2   HOW DO YOU FIND THE TRUTH?

In my experience, most litigants believe that the court process is all about finding out the truth and that, when the truth comes out at trial, they will be vindicated and will win. I have rarely met a litigant who did not believe that justice and the truth were on their side. In the vast majority of cases, both sides believe that, if only the truth were known, they would win the lawsuit for sure.

This plays out no less at mediation. People are not prepared to look at options that recognise a version of the facts other than their own. They tell me that they would prefer to go to court so the truth can come out.

There are four versions of the facts in every lawsuit. There is the claimant's version, the defendant's version, the version the judge finds to have occurred and there is what actually happened (the truth). The only one of these versions of the facts that is irrelevant in litigation is the truth. The other three all play a role. Focusing on the truth does not help disputants make an informed decision. They need to focus on what they will argue, what the other side will argue, and what the judge might decide, regardless of the truth. Once they acknowledge that the judge could make a decision based on facts that are not the truth, they can analyse possible settlement options and make informed decisions about avoiding the risk of having the judge decide.

It Happened at Mediation

A priest was suing his former church. He had been recruited from Europe to work in Canada, and he alleged that he was promised that the church would pay for the private education of his children and that he would have a job for life. The church representatives argued that those promises were never made.

We spent a significant amount of time in the mediation talking about whether or not the promises were made, and it became clear that there were different recollections of what had been promised, and both sides were adamant that theirs was the truthful version.

I suggested to the disputants that only God knows the truth and, unfortunately, God is not a witness who testifies at trial. Each side will present its version of the facts and the judge will make a factual determination of whether a promise of employment for life was made and whether the church undertook to pay for the education of the priest's children. Whatever conclusion the judge reaches, the facts will always be the facts and the truth will always be the truth. Unfortunately, we cannot guarantee that the judge will discover the truth. The disputants therefore needed to assess any settlement proposal based on what might happen in court, not on the 'truth' and their assessment of a just result.

The case settled.

10.3   NEED FOR MORE INFORMATION

One of the most common reasons I hear as to why people are not prepared to settle at mediation is that they believe they need more information to make an informed decision. Mediation is often held before oral and sometimes before documentary discovery, and lawyers believe that they cannot properly advise their clients on the appropriateness of particular settlement offers because they do not have enough information.

It is true that there are some cases for which settlement is not appropriate without more information. Personal injury and medical malpractice cases are examples of the types of disputes in which the lawyers and disputants need time to gather facts with which to reach an informed decision. It often takes time for injuries to manifest themselves. Not always, though.

In the vast majority of cases, lawyers can give an informed opinion and do a risk assessment early in the litigation process. We need to recognise at the outset that it is the extremely rare case where lawyers have full information on which to make an assessment, at any stage in the litigation process. Lawyers never know, for example, how their witnesses will hold up under cross-examination, what surprises will come up at trial, or how the judge will react to certain evidence. Lawyers do assessments all of the time for clients on the likelihood of success at trial, based on the information that they have.

Settling early in the litigation process only requires the lawyers to do the kind of risk assessment they are continually called upon to do.

If the disputants decide not to settle at an early stage so that the lawyers can gather more information and better assess their cases and advise their clients, there are three possibilities for each disputant and one certainty. One possibility is that the lawyer will obtain information that will change the current assessment and make his or her client's case stronger than the lawyer had previously believed. The second possibility is that the lawyer will obtain information that changes the assessment of the case to make it weaker than the lawyer first believed. The third possibility is that, with more information, the lawyer will do a risk assessment and the case will be no better and no worse than the assessment before. (Incidentally, a likely scenario is that, after more information is disclosed, both sides believe that their case is stronger and the disputants are no closer to agreeing on a settlement.)

The one certainty is that obtaining information will take time and cost money: time that could be better spent on more productive endeavours and money that could either be used to facilitate a settlement to be used for other purposes.

Only one of the three possibilities would justify a decision to defer settlement discussions until more information is obtained. Even then, only where the case was so much better after obtaining the information (and the other disputant was persuaded that the case was better) would it justify the extra expense and time of going through the process. For all other scenarios, it would make more sense to try to settle early.

It Happened at Mediation

I was mediating a wrongful dismissal case, and the mediation took place just one month after the employee had been dismissed. The disputants were trying to determine a fair amount for the former employer to pay the former employee as compensation for the dismissal. There was consensus that the employer should have provided notice (or pay in lieu of notice) that was sufficient to give the employee reasonable time to find another job. There was also consensus that a reasonable period of time would have been 10–12 months. One of the issues in the litigation would have been whether the employee had mitigated her damages (ie, reduced the amount that would have been owing by making all reasonable efforts to find alternative employment).

The disputants did not know whether the employee would find other work in one month, six months or one year. The employer suggested that the employee would find work immediately, and the employee thought that it would take her about a year.

The employee was prepared to assess the risk that she would not find other employment and was prepared to accept payment of eight months' salary. The employer refused, on the advice of its lawyer, on the basis that it needed more information to assess the likelihood that the employee would find alternative employment. The employer insisted on adjourning the mediation for 11 months and the employee reluctantly agreed.

When we reconvened, the employee had not found a job and there were no prospects that she would find one in the near future. The employer suggested that she had not searched properly, but the bottom line was that she did not have a job. Further, both sides had spent more money in the litigation process. The employee was no longer prepared to accept eight months' pay as a settlement and insisted on receiving 12 months' pay. The case settled with her receiving 11 months' pay.

The employer would have been better off assessing the risk of her not finding employment at the first mediation, and paying her the eight months' pay she was then requesting.

There are other situations where it clearly makes sense to postpone the mediation until more information is available.

It Happened at Mediation

The dispute was between a bank and a former business customer. The customer had borrowed a significant amount of money personally and through a business, and was unable to repay either loan. A few years before the mediation, the bank and the business customer were able to work out an agreement whereby the bank agreed to forego some of the interest on the business loan and the customer agreed on a payment schedule for repayment of the principal amount owing on the business loan. The customer assumed that the personal loan was forgiven as part of the package, and stopped making payments on it. The bank assumed that the money borrowed with the personal loan was still owing, and sued the customer for the amount owing on the personal loan.

There was a dispute about what had specifically been said during the negotiations concerning the new terms for repayment of the business loan. The people at the bank who had negotiated the agreement respecting the business loan had since left the bank, though the documents did not suggest that there was forgiveness of the personal loan.

The disputants at the mediation debated the issue of whether the settlement related to the personal loan and, of course, could not agree. The bank employee who had originally negotiated the loan could be reached, and the bank said that, if this person confirmed that there was forgiveness of the personal loan, the bank would not pursue the litigation. In the circumstances, it did make sense to adjourn so that the bank could consult with its former employee. After the consultation, we had a second mediation session and the dispute was settled.

10.4   USING OBJECTIVE CRITERIA

Nobody likes to be taken advantage of in a mediation. People seek results that they perceive as fair. One of the challenges in selecting the viable or workable option is to look for objective criteria, standards of fairness, that both sides can accept as being objectively fair. Objective criteria change the discussion from one where both sides advocate their own view as the right outcome to one where there is resort to an external standard. Objective criteria help people to move away from the subjectivity that pervades disputes, and towards something that is perceived as legitimate.

There are many examples of objective criteria, and they vary depending on what is to be valued. They can range from prices paid and received for similar items, and amounts paid in similar disputes, to independent valuations. It may be that the best objective criterion is one that is left to an independent person, where the disputants do not know what the person will determine as fair.

It Happened at Mediation

I was mediating a dispute between a landlord and a commercial tenant. The lease had a renewal clause that the tenant had exercised. The clause stated that the landlord and tenant should attempt to agree on a rent for the renewal period and, if they could not agree, they should go to binding arbitration. They could not agree and, before proceeding to an expensive and protracted arbitration, they decided to attempt a mediation.

After finding some creative options to overcome some obstacles, they had repaired what was a damaged relationship, and had the task of coming up with rent for the next five-year period. They could not agree on what equivalent properties would rent for. They could agree, however, on a particular real estate valuer in their city for whom they both had respect. They therefore settled on the basis that they would go to the valuer, ask for an inexpensive valuation (certainly less expensive than the anticipated cost of the arbitration), and agree to pay and receive whatever the valuer determined was fair. They also decided that they would set high and low parameters so that if the valuer chose a figure outside the parameters, they would only go to the parameter.

10.5   MAKING THE FIRST OFFER

A concern for many disputants in mediation is who should make the first offer and what should that offer be. In my experience (both through surveys and through observation), the vast majority of people prefer to receive rather than make the first offer. That is understandable. They believe that, if they make the first offer, they may give too much and the other side will accept immediately; they may offer too little and the other side will be insulted and leave the mediation; they may lose the opportunity to learn from the other side as it makes its first offer; and they will lose the opportunity to assess the other side's offer to determine whether it is reasonable and whether, therefore, a deal is likely.

There are, however, advantages to making the first offer. The person who makes the first offer is able to take control of the negotiation and set its parameters by defining appropriate ranges, rather than reacting to them; the disputants can avoid the time that is so often wasted while both sides wait for the other to make the first offer; and the person making the first offer demonstrates confidence that can affect other aspects of the negotiation.

The person making the first offer should try to do so in a way that does not cause the other person to walk out, and does not give away too much. Resorting to objective criteria can satisfy both of these objectives. If the offer is presented not as the final or only answer, but as one that is based on objective criteria, it will be difficult for the other person to get angry and leave the mediation. Also, if it is based on objective criteria and if the other side accepts it, that will probably be a good result.

Few people, however, accept the first offer that is made. They usually like to play the negotiation dance. That is why it makes sense to make a first offer that is based on objective criteria, but is not the best offer that the person can make. Later offers should, where possible, also be based on objective criteria.

10.6   SHUTTLE DIPLOMACY

While some mediators conduct the entire mediation in joint session, most resort to caucus (a private meeting), where the mediator shuttles between (or among) the disputants, presenting offers and counter-offers in the hope that the disputants can reach agreement. Is that a good thing? In caucus, the disputants have an opportunity to consider what is presented, discuss it and decide whether to counter-offer. They usually feel more comfortable having their discussions in private, and they usually prefer the mediator to make the offer for them.

Most mediators present offers in a positive light, in the way that the person making the offer would want the offer to be presented. That is not to suggest, though, that mediators try to 'sell' offers. They will discuss with disputants the benefits (and problems) with particular offers and the options for response. There can often be many rounds of offer and counter-offer. It is not uncommon for the mediator to present one side's offer, and for the other side to react angrily, threaten to end the mediation and then make a counter-offer. The shuttle diplomacy process can go on for several hours.

The basis upon which each side generates offers may be very different, and the analysis that each side applies to offers may also vary, but that does not prevent a settlement from being reached. While the mediator will almost always attempt to explain the basis upon which an offer was made, the person receiving the offer need not accept the basis to accept the offer.

It Happened at Mediation

A homeowner had incurred significant property damage during a storm, and was suing her insurance company to compensate her for the damage. The homeowner was convinced that her electronic items (TV, stereo, computer, etc) had been irreparably damaged by the storm and that she was therefore entitled to compensation for that loss. The insurance company was convinced that the electronic equipment was old and that regular wear and tear could explain any perceived damage.

On the other hand, the insurance company accepted that damage had been done to the homeowner's deck.

In formulating offers, the insurance company could not justify paying for the electronics, but could justify paying for the deck; the homeowner insisted on receiving money for the electronics.

Rather than explain the justification for each offer, therefore, I asked each side to look at the total amount being offered and allocate it however they believed it should most appropriately be allocated. The two sides eventually agreed on a cash amount and didn't have to agree on allocation.

10.7   NUMEROUS OPTIONS

During the shuttle diplomacy process, the mediator may ask disputants to consider making a number of offers simultaneously. While at first blush this may seem to be a waste of time (after all, why not explore one option to see if it is workable before proceeding to other options), it can be a creative and efficient way to arrive at a solution. The mediator will ask disputants to come up with two or more options that they would be prepared to accept to settle the dispute. The mediator will then ask them to put the options in the form of simultaneous offers and be prepared to reach agreement if the other disputant accepts any of the offers.

The disputant receiving the offers can choose to accept or pursue the option that best meets that disputant's interests. This will allow the disputants to focus on the path that is most likely to lead to resolution, and not waste time exploring options that don't satisfy interests.

It Happened at Mediation

In a wrongful dismissal case, the claimant mentioned in the storytelling that he had loved working for the company and, if at all possible, would like to return to work there. The company acknowledged that the employee had been good at his work, but that it did not want to rehire him.

In caucus with the employee, we discussed him coming back to work for the employer and the compensation for the employee if he did not return to work for the employer. The employee preferred the option that would have allowed him to return to work, but recognised that it might not be feasible. The employee decided to make two parallel offers: one involving a small payment and return to work; the other involving a larger payment.

The defendant (employer) balked at the large payment and agreed to continue the discussion on the two parallel tracks. It counter-offered a smaller lump sum payment or a return to work with no payment.

The employee gladly accepted the offer to return to work in return for agreeing to forego damages for wrongful dismissal.

10.8   WHEN IS IT THE END?

One of the most difficult things for disputants to determine is when they are reaching the end of the shuttle diplomacy process and when an offer should be accepted. Disputants want to know when they are reaching the end so that they can make a final concession to get a deal done. They do not want to make their final concession too early. In theory, the end should arrive whenever it arrives, but in practice, it is not so clear.

One of the ways of knowing that the end is approaching is that time is running out at the mediation. When a conclusion time has been set, the disputants and lawyers know that the mediation will end at a particular time. As the deadline approaches, disputants get a sense of urgency and make final concessions.

Another way is for the mediator to signal to the disputants that the other disputants are feeling that they have reached their limit (either monetarily or emotionally). As the mediator is in the room with both (or all) disputants, the mediator can get a sense of whether the disputants are feeling pushed and whether they have a lot of stamina for a few more rounds of negotiation.

10.9   IT'S A 'FINAL OFFER'

During the process of selecting the options, the mediator will often hear disputants or their lawyers suggest that an offer is a 'bottom line' or a 'final offer'. Sometimes, when a disputant makes a final offer, he or she is not prepared to offer anything else. On other occasions, however, the 'final offer' is a bargaining tool used in an attempt to get the other side to agree to what is being proposed. In yet other circumstances, a final offer is made with the full intention of sticking to it, but circumstances (and new information) cause the person making the final offer to reconsider and make another offer. In any of those cases, a final offer is certainly a sign that the mediation is close to an end.

As a mediator, I will always disclose that a disputant has stated that a particular offer is a final offer or a bottom line. It is then left to the person receiving the offer to assess its finality.

10.10 SHOULD LAWYERS ASK THE MEDIATOR TO LEAVE THE ROOM WHEN ASSESSING OFFERS?

There are some situations in caucus where the lawyers wonder whether it is appropriate to have candid discussions with their clients in the presence of the mediator. Some are comfortable talking in front of the mediator, while others prefer the mediator to leave the room. Having discussions with the mediator present can help the mediator understand the issues better and give him or her a sense of how far the disputant will bend during the mediation process. This information can be helpful to the mediator in attempting to broker a deal.

On the other hand, if the mediator has a sense of how far one disputant will go, the mediator may not approach the caucus with the other side with the same vigour as he or she otherwise would. In addition, a disputant may not speak candidly to his or her lawyer if the mediator is present. Also, the lawyer may want to say some things that are hard for the client to hear, and may not want to do so in front of the mediator.

There is nothing wrong with disputants and lawyers asking a mediator to leave the room. The mediator should not feel insulted and should respect the request that has been made.

It Happened at Mediation

Some lawyers believe that they should control the mediation and fear giving control to the mediator. A woman was injured in an accident at a hospital while visiting her husband and sued the hospital for damages. While I encouraged the woman who was injured to participate in the storytelling, her lawyer told me that he would prefer her not to speak and that he speak for her. He then told me that, if I did not mind, he would like some time to speak directly to his client in private. I told him that he was certainly entitled to speak to his client in private and that I did not mind at all.

After a half hour or so, he called me in and told me that he and his client had formulated an offer and that they wanted me to present the offer. He then began to review it with me. When I questioned him about some of the aspects of the offer, he became a bit agitated and told me to just present it exactly as he was presenting it to me. Since I was unclear about some of the terms of the offer, I suggested that he come with me for the presentation, which he did.

The insurance company made a counter-offer that I presented to the lawyer and his client. He again asked me to leave the room and only called me back once he and his client had agreed on a specific offer. This pattern was repeated four times and a deal was eventually reached.

While I was frustrated through the process, it did result in agreement and the disputants were pleased with the result. There are times when it makes sense to discuss issues and offers with the mediator in caucus, and there are other times when the disputants and lawyers work more effectively without the mediator.

10.11   REALITY TESTING

As I stated earlier, the test for disputants is not whether they can reach an agreement that is the perfect or even the fair solution; the test is whether they can reach an agreement that is better for both (or all) disputants than their respective BATNAs. Part of the role of the mediator is to help the disputants assess, in caucus, what will happen if they do not reach agreement. Lawyers can help their clients understand the consequences of not reaching agreement.

Reality testing (discussing what will happen if a deal is not reached) is common in caucuses when disputants are considering offers. If the dispute is in the context of litigation, the disputants need to consider, for example, the likely outcome if the matter is to proceed to trial. Litigation is, by nature, unpredictable. It is inherently difficult for lawyers to assess objectively the likely outcome of a trial.

First, not all facts are known to both sides. Secondly, it may be difficult to predict which facts a judge will accept and which facts a judge will reject. Thirdly, and perhaps most importantly, lawyers tend consistently to overvalue their own cases, no matter how hard they try not to. This is not meant as a criticism; it is simply stated as an observation. Proof is that, in every mediation I have ever conducted, the lawyers' estimates of their own client's chances of success have been higher than the other side's estimate. At least one of the estimates is therefore always wrong, if not both. Lawyers tend to prefer their own client's version of facts and focus on the facts that support their client's claims, rather than the facts that do not.

Reality testing also involves clients thinking about the time that it will take for the matter to be determined, either at trial or elsewhere, and the likely cost of the process. They should consider the potential additional costs if they are unsuccessful at trial and are required to pay the other side's legal costs and the potential additional costs and time of a potential appeal. They should also think about the time that they and others in their organisation are spending dealing with the litigation rather than the things they enjoy (or are profitable). The litigation may also be causing them stress.

Although most disputants are informed by their lawyers of the potential downside to continuing with litigation, they may not have considered these as factors that should cause them to accept a settlement offer that would otherwise be unacceptable.

It is the mediator's role to discuss the litigation process with each of the disputants in private session, to talk with them about the fact that a judge could find against them, and to help them compare the offer that has been presented to the anticipated advantages and disadvantages of taking the matter to trial.

That is not to say that it is always right to reach an agreement at mediation and always wrong to leave without an agreement. There are situations in which it makes more sense to go to the BATNA rather than reach an agreement. Take the case where the retired doctor rented a car and wanted to return it before the lease had expired. The leasing company wanted to give experience to a new in-house lawyer and the doctor wanted to represent himself at trial. It made more sense for both sides to go to court rather than settle.

Most disputants want mediators to help them try to settle their disputes and mediators should and will try to help them examine all options and compare those options to their BATNAs. In the end, however, it is for the disputants to compare any offer to their BATNA and make the appropriate choice.

Tips for Lawyers

- Disputes can be extremely emotional. To the extent that the other disputant needs to have an ego massaged, to be told how good they are, and to be understood and appreciated, there are opportunities to get better deals. After hearing that their concerns are understood and that they are appreciated, the other disputant may be more likely to make substantive concessions. In a wrongful dismissal case, for example, it may be beneficial for the company to tell the former employee how much he or she was appreciated and what a good job the employee did, and not focus on the few things that former employee did that the company did not like. I have even seen an experienced lawyer persuade their client that the company should host a retirement party for the former employee. These gestures cost nothing or very little, and can heal a wound. Dealing with the emotional issues first can sometimes free individuals to focus on settlement and make concessions.

- Some negotiators take extreme positions in mediation and make many concessions. Others say that they are 'cutting to the chase' and start with what they believe will be the final solution. In my experience, neither approach is the best. After creative options have been explored and it is time to make offers, the best negotiators start with an offer that is objectively justifiable, is reasonable and is fair. The offer should leave room, however, for the negotiation dance. Most disputants believe that if they do not force the other side to make concessions and participate in the negotiation dance, they have not negotiated effectively and not reached a good deal. While this is not necessarily logical, it is often true.

- Making the first offer can be an effective strategy in mediation. It can set the range for future offers and can jumpstart a stalled process.

- It is a myth that complex cases cannot settle at mediation early in the litigation process and need more time and more information. Try not to fall into the trap of assuming that you need more information. In order to give your client advice about settling, you need to do a risk assessment based on the information that you have. No risk assessment is perfect. Taking time to gather more information may result in your (and the other side's) assessment of your client's case changing for the better, for the worse, or not at all. The one certainty is that it will cost the clients money and take time to get the information.

- Be careful with your use of the terms 'final offer' or 'bottom line'. The best lawyers only use these terms at the very end of the mediation, when it is clear that their clients can go no further. Even then, the term should be used with caution. The danger with using a term such as 'final offer' is that, after presenting this, your client may be persuaded to make a further concession. It will then appear that you were not being honest in your categorisation of the final offer and you may not be trusted in the future.

- There may be times in the mediation where you want to discuss things with your client without the mediator present. If that happens, just ask the mediator to leave for a few moments while you have some private discussions with your client.

- When a mediation turns into a shuttle diplomacy about money, it is a relatively safe assumption that there will come a time when each side will be asked to split the difference between the latest offers. Lawyers, knowing this, should keep this fact in mind when making and receiving offers.

- Before making an offer, you will, of course, need to confirm with your client that the client commits to making the offer. Similarly, when an offer is made to your client, and the offer is rejected, you will need to confirm that the client has rejected the offer. Some lawyers have forms that clients sign prior to making offers confirming their authorisation to make the offer, and other sheets that clients sign when they reject (or accept) offers from the other side.

Tips for Mediators

- After disputants have brainstormed options they will look to you to help them choose from among the options. This is often an appropriate time in the mediation for shuttle diplomacy.

- At the commencement of the first caucus with each disputant, it may be helpful to restate the ground rules relating to confidentiality so that there is no misunderstanding.

- When you have a caucus with one of the disputants, it is helpful to give the other disputant a task to complete while they are waiting for you to conclude the first caucus. You can ask them to consider how some of the options that have been brainstormed could be combined to produce an option that may be viable to all (or both) disputants, for example.

- If you have spent a long time in caucus with one disputant and need more time, you may want to break from that caucus to let the others know that you need more time and that you will meet with them shortly. That way, they will not be wondering what is going on.

- If you are involved in a shuttle diplomacy mediation where you are asked to present offers, try to present them as though the person making the offer were standing next to you. You must be careful not to suggest that there is more to come or that the offer is not the best one. At the same time, you should not suggest that an offer is a final or best offer unless that has been made clear to you. If an offer is presented to you as a final offer, you should present it as such.

- Disputants can explore more than one option at a time. They may make simultaneous offers about which they are indifferent and allow the other side to choose the option that it prefers. If one side makes simultaneous offers, you may want to encourage the other side to respond with simultaneous offers. The benefit of simultaneous offers is that they allow the people receiving them to select the one that best meets their interests.

- There may be times where the offer you are asked to present is confusing or is one that you are not comfortable presenting. In those circumstances, you may want to ask the lawyer or disputant to come with you to present the offer so that you can make sure that it is clear and presented in its most positive light.

- When a lawyer presents an offer to you in caucus that he or she wants you to present to the other side, you may want to check with the client informally to make sure that the client agrees to make the offer and knows that he or she will be committed to the offer if it is accepted.

CHAPTER 11

OVERCOMING OBSTACLES

Marathon runners talk about 'hitting the wall', the point in the marathon where they find that they are so tired that they believe they cannot go any farther. They must summon up all of their strength and find a way, any way, to get past the wall.

Most mediations also hit the wall. There comes a point where someone is threatening to leave, where bottom lines have been exchanged and they do not show a zone of agreement, or where one side is being obstinate and will not move from a fixed position. How can mediators overcome the obstacles, break down the wall, and deal with some of the difficulties? How do they deal with personal attacks, people who lie, or people who threaten to walk out? How should they deal with lawyers who just do not want to settle? What if there are many issues and disputants cannot agree on what to do about the first issue without knowing what will happen for other issues?

11.1 PERSONAL ATTACKS

Disputes are often emotional. It should not surprise us, therefore, that people in mediations engage in personal attacks, usually against each other, and sometimes against the mediator.

It Happened at Mediation

I vividly remember the first case that I ever mediated. The dispute was among a board of a self-regulating profession. The board had split into two factions and the factions were so angry with each other that they would not stay in the same room. The entire mediation was conducted through caucus (a private meeting) and shuttle diplomacy. It was late in the day and I was in a caucus with one of the sides and one member of the board was becoming more and more frustrated with me. Finally she said, 'How many mediations have you conducted, anyway?'. My nightmare question. I had no idea what to say until finally (after stumbling for a few seconds), I realised that she probably did not care about me or my experience; she was probably concerned about how my experience would result in her getting a worse deal in the mediation. I must have said something that had upset her.

I therefore suggested to her that there must have been something that I had said or done to make her think that I did not have the requisite experience and I asked her what it was. She was very happy to tell me all of the things that she disliked about the way that I was mediating and she was anxious to give me suggestions about how I might deal with the other side to achieve a better solution. Fortunately for me, the discussion never got back to my experience.

Personal attacks are usually the result of people being upset and thinking that blame is the solution. The emotion has to be recognised (either by the mediator or by the other disputant) in order for the person to feel heard. Interactive listening skills (discussed earlier in Chapter 7, 'Determining Interests') therefore come in handy when there are personal attacks. The person doing the attacking will need to be assured that the others in the room want to listen to the person's concerns.

When people feel attacked, they do not usually listen well. They usually need to be heard before they can listen. The challenge that can be put to the person doing the attacking is: can you find a way to express your concerns, without using the words that make it difficult for the other person to listen? If you can, you are more likely to achieve your objectives.

11.2   PEOPLE LYING IN MEDIATION

Posturing at mediation is common; lying is rare. Unfortunately, the line between posturing and lying is not always clear. One can expect posturing, including people saying that positions are 'final' or that 'bottom lines' have been reached.

A lie is a statement that is untrue, where the person making the statement knows it is untrue, and the statement is intended to mislead others into taking courses of action they would not take if they knew the real facts. A deliberate intention to mislead about facts is not acceptable.

A decision not to disclose information may or may not be a lie. People in a negotiation have a right, to a limit, to decide what they do and do not want to disclose, and that right is no less valid in a mediation. If the failure to disclose suggests to the other disputant facts that are untrue, if there is a failure to disclose information that is material and legally must be disclosed, or if the non-disclosure reaches the level of a fraud, however, a non-disclosure could be a lie.

An agreement that is based on a lie or based on fraud may be voidable, and would certainly damage any relationship that might exist. A mediator who knows of a lie and allows the lie to be told could be a participant in the fraud.

If a mediator discovers that lies are being told in the mediation, the mediator will either need to have the disputants correct the misunderstanding or terminate the mediation.

If the mediator (or a lawyer) learns in a confidential caucus that one of the disputants is about to lie to the other, the situation is more complex. The mediator has a duty to keep the information confidential, but neither the lawyer nor the mediator can participate in a fraud.

The lawyer and mediator should first try to negotiate with the disputant who is about to lie and attempt to persuade him or her that it would be a mistake. The disputant should be told that an agreement based on a lie may be voidable and the lie may not, therefore, have its intended effect. The mediator may then work with the disputant who wants to lie to discuss the interests behind the desire to lie, to find out if there is a way to proceed that accomplishes the disputant's goals in an ethically acceptable way.

If the disputant cannot be convinced not to lie, the mediator and the lawyer may refuse to continue to participate in the mediation. If the mediator ends the mediation, he or she must do so in a way that does not suggest to the other disputant why the mediation has ended.

11.3 THREATENING TO WALK OUT

Some disputants believe that an effective strategy is to threaten to walk out of the mediation. They believe that will convince the other side that they are serious and may force compromise.

In my experience, threatening to walk out of the mediation is not effective. It only persuades the other side of the unreasonableness of the person threatening to walk out.

Threats usually lead to more threats, and the mediation may become a battle of who can walk out first. It is often left to the mediator to calm the disputants and help them to see the benefits of staying to talk. The mediator can explain that, if a disputant does walk out, it is not the mediator who is harmed, as the mediator will go on to his or her next case; it is the disputants that will leave the mediation without a settlement. The mediator will certainly want to find out why the person threatening to walk out wants to end the mediation. Perhaps that person's interests can be addressed in the mediation better than they can be in litigation.

In the end, however, if people want to walk out, I let them walk out. It is their dispute and they have the right to terminate the mediation if they believe mediation will not accomplish their goals.

11.4 LAWYERS WHO DO NOT WANT TO SETTLE

Most lawyers see the benefits of mediation and many embrace it; a few lawyers, however, are not mediation supporters and fight the process, believing that it adds extra cost (and, in some cases, reduces lawyers' fees). Lawyers who embrace the mediation process will have to deal with lawyers who do not, and mediators will have to deal with both groups. There are a number of techniques that mediators and lawyers can use to deal with those who do not want to participate in the mediation.

It can often help to allow obstreperous lawyers to vent their feelings and present their positions. These lawyers may feel the need to posture in front of their clients and allowing this is rarely harmful. If they feel that letting off steam has accomplished its purpose (helping the other side to understand what they will be arguing at trial), they may be more amenable during the balance of the process. A lot of interactive listening can therefore be helpful.

It may be helpful to ask difficult lawyers to assist in some way, perhaps with the interpretation of a point of law. Some lawyers may fear mediation because they are concerned that they do not add sufficient value to it (though they will not tell you this explicitly). If they feel they are useful to the process, they may participate constructively.

It may be helpful to speak directly to lawyers who appear to want to disrupt the process, without their clients present. The lawyers may be posturing in front of their clients and may feel free to talk openly in a meeting without clients. These lawyers may even be open to discussing settlement options that they may not have been prepared to discuss with clients present.

It Happened at Mediation

I was mediating a case between a company and a former employee where the employee alleged constructive dismissal. Throughout the joint sessions and the caucuses, the lawyers for each side insisted that they were right in law and would win the constructive dismissal argument.

After unsuccessfully trying a number of techniques to help them explore options and perhaps even make offers, I decided to bring the lawyers together without their clients. Initially, they continued their arguments about the merits of their cases. The discussion then turned to the amount that the company might contribute in any settlement toward the former employee's legal costs. It was during this discussion that the lawyer for the employee explained that she was the second lawyer for the employee, that the original lawyer was a friend of the former employee, and the original lawyer had extremely high outstanding legal bills. The lawyer had felt uncomfortable discussing this issue in front of her client.

The lawyers realised that the key issue in dispute was not the constructive dismissal issue and damages associated with it, but rather an allocation for legal costs. I helped the lawyers discuss the issue and they agreed to recommend to their clients an amount for damages and have a third party look at the legal costs incurred, determine an appropriate amount for costs and allocate the amount between the two lawyers who had worked for the employee. That was the basis of the settlement, and the issue would never have arisen but for the private discussion with the lawyers.

11.5   REACTIVE DEVALUATION

We all like to have our offer accepted; nobody likes to accept what the other side proposes. When trust has dissipated from a relationship, we assume that everything the other side does or offers is to our detriment. Groucho Marx famously proclaimed that he would never join a club that would admit him as a member.

In negotiation, this plays out by having each of the disputants believe that they cannot accept what the other side has proposed, even if the proposal is a good one. They devalue what the other side is offering and make a counter-offer so that they do not have to accept something from the person they do not trust. They believe that, if the other disputant has made an offer, he or she must be prepared to offer more. This is what is known as reactive devaluation: devaluing what the other side has offered just because the other side has offered it. The difficulty with reactive devaluation, of course, is that if both (or all) sides to a dispute engage in it, nobody ever says yes.

The first step in overcoming reactive devaluation is recognising that it exists. Mediators may choose to remind disputants about it in mediation if they believe it is occurring. Disputants who recognise it have the difficult task of trying to put out of their minds the fact that something has been proposed by the other side, so that they can make a realistic assessment of it. If a deal is to be reached, someone has to say yes to what the other side has offered.

It Happened at Mediation

Two retired men had decided to go into business together to develop some land. One contributed the land and the other contributed capital. A dispute arose about their relative contributions and how to divide the profits (if any) so they came to mediation.

These men had been friends for many years but, because of all the acrimony relating to the development, they now hated each other. One of the options we explored was one man buying the other out. The difficulty was that, whenever an offer was made, the person receiving the offer got very angry, talked about how unreasonable the other person had been, and threatened to walk out. Neither side was willing to look objectively at an offer.

We then explored the possibility of dividing the land and allowing each to keep and develop a portion of it on his own. As there was a logical dividing line, neither side felt that it was 'the other side's offer' and this idea was tentatively accepted. A difficulty arose, however, because, once the land was divided, each man would have certain financial obligations over the next year in relation to the other's land. One of the men (the first) demanded that the other post a letter of credit until the obligations were complete. The second man refused and said that the first man should post a letter of credit.

Both men wanted to win and, perhaps more importantly, wanted the other side to lose. Each firmly believed that he should not post a letter of credit, but that the other should. In the circumstances, it was not practical for either man to post a letter of credit.

In the end, both men were tired and both men wanted a deal. I talked with each of them about reactive devaluation and they both recognised that it was occurring. They decided that a deal even without a letter of credit was better than no deal at all. They both realised that there were strong incentives for each side to honour obligations and consequences for not honouring the obligations, and they agreed to settle without letters of credit being posted.

11.6   DISPUTANTS LOSE TRUST IN THE MEDIATOR

There are situations where, for whatever reason, one or both of the disputants lose confidence in the mediator's ability to facilitate the discussion. If either the lawyers or the mediator perceives that this is the case, the issue should be discussed with the person who may have lost faith in the mediator.

There could be a communication problem (perhaps one of the mediator's comments was misunderstood, for example). In those situations, the issue can be discussed and usually resolved.

The concern may, however, be one that cannot be overcome through discussion with the mediator. In that case, it may be appropriate for the lawyer to ask for a caucus with the mediator, tell him or her that there is a problem and that perhaps the disputants should engage a new mediator. The objective for everyone at the mediation is to determine whether there is a solution that is better for both disputants than proceeding to court. If that can best be achieved by employing a different mediator, then a different mediator should be employed.

11.7 MULTIPLE ISSUES: THE ONE TEXT

In some disputes, there is only one issue. In others, there are multiple issues. The traditional approach to dealing with multiple issues is to examine one issue at a time and try to resolve that issue before moving on. Unfortunately, that is not always the most successful approach, as it often results in no agreement being reached. People need to know what they are getting in an overall agreement before they can make concessions on a single issue. This is true even where the issues are not connected.

In *Getting to Yes*,[1] the authors talk about a mediation approach known as 'one text' to help resolve disputes that have numerous issues. The one text approach involves a more active approach by the mediator than the conventional mediation, and requires the mediator to make some value judgments.

After setting the table, storytelling, the determination of interests, and the brainstorming of options, the mediator (or mediation team) will take some time to draft a possible settlement agreement that balances the views expressed on the different issues, and takes into account the interests that have been presented. The objective for the mediator is not to get the answer exactly right, but rather to produce a skeleton draft agreement from which the disputants can work.

The draft is then presented to each of the disputants in caucus, and they are not asked whether they like the draft or would be prepared to accept it as an agreement. They are asked which parts of the draft do not satisfy their interests and why. The mediator (or team) then takes the information and uses it to produce a second draft of the one text. The second draft is then presented to the disputants for their analysis to determine what parts of that draft do not satisfy their interests and why.

This process (of gathering information and producing new drafts) is repeated until the mediator believes that no purpose would be served by creating a further draft. At that point, the final draft is given to the disputants and they are not asked what they like and do not like, but rather whether they would be prepared to accept the agreement, as drafted, in its entirety. They will be able to make informed assessments of what they will be receiving in the agreement and what they will be giving up. They will know that, if they do not accept, the mediation will be at an end and, if both sides accept, there will be a deal.

The advantage of using one text is that it allows everyone to know what they will be giving up and what they will be getting in relation to all of the issues before committing.

It Happened at Mediation

I was co-mediating a dispute with one of my partners. The dispute involved a group of manufacturers and a group of customers. The two sides were trying to come up with prices for numerous products, delivery terms and other conditions. We initially had discussions about the numerous issues, and it became clear that this was not simply a dispute about price. We decided to use a one text approach.

---

1   Fisher, R, Ury, W and Patton, B, *Getting to Yes: Negotiating Agreement Without Giving In*, 2nd edn, 1991, New York: Penguin Books.

During the evening of the first day, my partner and I drafted a discussion document (our first draft of the one text) based on the comments that had been made during the day and our understanding of the disputants' interests. I presented the document to one side and my partner to the other side. Neither side liked the document and both had numerous suggestions for improvement. My partner and I met later that day and told each other what we had learned from each group. We then prepared a second draft and presented the new draft to the two groups, though this time we switched groups. The reason for the switch was that we did not want to become associated with one group or the other, and we each wanted to have an opportunity to hear from both groups.

We met again later that day and created a third draft. We learned, for example, that some of the changes we made in the second draft created more problems than they solved, and we reverted to some of the language from the first draft.

Once we had reached draft number seven, we believed that there were no further ways we could balance the interests and we told the disputants we had done the best we could. Both sides accepted the deal.

Tips for Lawyers

- If the other side engages in a personal attack on you or your client, you may want to ask for a caucus to discuss the issue with the mediator. If possible, you should try to stay out of personal attacks, as they usually end in both sides losing. It can sometimes be helpful to suggest to the other side that a series of personal attacks can only lead to antagonism and entrenchment of positions.

- Lying in mediation is unethical and is contrary to codes of professional conduct for lawyers. That does not require you to fully disclose weaknesses in your case nor does it prevent you from posturing; it does require you not to say or do something that you know to be untrue or that is designed to mislead the other side.

- Beware of getting caught in a game of reactive devaluation. An offer is not a bad one solely by virtue of the fact that it is made by the other disputant. There is nothing wrong with accepting an offer from the other side if it is a good offer. In fact, accepting the other side's offer can help improve a relationship by showing the other side that you trust them and have been persuaded by them.

- Think carefully before making threats. Threats usually lead to counter-threats. Even threatening to walk out of the mediation can cause the other side to get upset and shift them from taking a co-operative approach to a competitive one. You can still make the other side aware of the consequences of its actions by talking about what may happen if the mediation breaks down, and suggesting that that would not be a good result for anyone, including your client.

- It is not bad to ask the mediator for a sense of how the other side is reacting to what is being proposed. The mediator will tell you unless the information is confidential. Knowing how the other side is reacting may give you a sense of how to proceed and what kind of offer to make.

- If you believe that a one text approach would be an effective way to resolve multiple issues in your dispute, you may recommend that the mediator try it.

Tips for Mediators

- If disputants are stuck, go back through the stages of the mediation process. Explore interests, brainstorm more options, look for objective criteria and allow for more storytelling. If there is an ongoing relationship between the disputants, focus on the relationship and the benefits to resolving the dispute amicably.

- If disputants (or lawyers) are engaging in personal attacks, you have a number of options: you can try to facilitate the communication to bring out the interests; you can break into caucus and discuss the attacks; you can try to refocus the attacks onto the problem.

- If disputants or lawyers lie to the other side and you know for certain that they have lied, you will want to call a caucus with the disputant who has lied to attempt to persuade him or her to tell the truth. If the disputant refuses, you will have to resign as mediator because you cannot be a party to a fraud. You will need to try to resign in a way that does not suggest to one disputant that the other has lied (perhaps saying, for example, that circumstances have arisen that make it impossible for you to continue as mediator). Note that posturing does not usually amount to lying.

- If disputants threaten to walk out of the mediation, don't be afraid to let them. I try not to force anyone to stay if they don't want to stay. It should be their decision whether to stay or terminate the mediation. However, I will ask them why they are walking out, what it is they are trying to achieve, and whether their goals are better met by ending the mediation or participating further in it.

- If there are multiple issues in the dispute, consider using the one text approach. That will require you to consider and balance all of the issues in a draft solution to the dispute. You can present the draft to each side, asking how they believe the draft could be improved to meet their interests. You will then try to produce a further draft that attempts to balance the interests that have been expressed. Continue the process until you believe that you cannot produce a better draft than the last one you have created. Ask the disputants whether they would be prepared to accept that draft if the other side accepted it as well. If either side does not accept, the mediation should end.

CHAPTER 12

POWER IMBALANCES

It is a rare mediation where the disputants come to the table with absolutely equal power. We recognise a power imbalance in mediation and, depending on our perspective, either take advantage of it or try to reduce it. In order to discuss power in mediation and effective ways of dealing with it, we first have to know what power is. Even if we can define it, what should we do if there is a power imbalance in the mediation? Is it the mediator's role to balance power? What if the power imbalance is so severe that the disempowered person cannot make an informed decision? What if there is a threat of violence? Are there safeguards that we can institute to make sure that power is not abused at mediation?

Most people have difficulty defining power: they know it when they see it but they don't have a definition for it. They will refer to the indicia of power, the characteristics or assets that they believe give people power. These might include money, knowledge, experience, position in an organisation, ability to communicate effectively, physical attributes, race and gender. Sometimes, though, someone with none of those characteristics has power. Those of us who negotiate with our young children know how frustrated we feel at times when we are in public and our child threatens to cry and scream if not given his or her way. While we may have the money, experience, knowledge, ability to communicate and physical attributes, we feel powerless.

Power, therefore, cannot be defined by its indicia, but it can be defined. One of the difficulties in defining power, I believe, lies in the fact that there are two types of power – substantive power and process power.

12.1   SUBSTANTIVE POWER

Substantive power is the type of power that we usually think of in negotiation; it is power that is inherent in a situation and exists regardless of how well we negotiate. Substantive power is measured by the disputants' perceptions of the strength of their respective BATNAs. As you will recall, a BATNA (Best Alternative to a Negotiated Agreement) is what you can do if an agreement is not reached. The better the course of action you can take if you do not reach an agreement, the more power you have. If both disputants believe during a negotiation that, if there is no resolution, person A will thrive and person B will go bankrupt, person A will have more substantive power than person B in the negotiation.

A disputant at a mediation should only accept a deal if that deal is better than what that disputant perceives his or her BATNA to be. If the person's BATNA is very good, the deal on the table will have to be extremely good for the person to accept it; on the other hand, if the person believes that he or she has a weak BATNA, the person will accept deals that are not as good because, otherwise, the person is stuck with a bad BATNA.

Improving the disputants' perceptions of their relative BATNAs therefore increases power in a negotiation.

Substantive power refers to the perception of BATNA rather than the actual BATNA because all that matters in determining power is the disputants' beliefs about what will happen if they don't reach agreement. It doesn't matter whether they are, in fact, right because it is the perception of what will happen that will influence their behaviour in the negotiation and cause them to make concessions or accept offers.

Most of the indicia of power listed above help people develop a good BATNA and therefore are perceived to create power. In some situations, however, where these indicia do not help create a better BATNA, they do not create power. In the situation with my child in public, for example, my perception is that, if my child screams, I will be embarrassed. We both perceive, on the other hand, that if my child screams, there will be no horrible adverse consequences to her. If I can change the perceptions so that my child perceives that she will be punished if she screams, we have changed our perceptions of our relative BATNAs and have therefore changed the power dynamic.

Substantive power is also a relative as opposed to an absolute concept. Everyone has a BATNA; therefore, everyone has some substantive power in the negotiation. When assessing power, we are comparing the consequences to each disputant of not reaching agreement, not determining how much power each disputant has on some absolute scale.

Substantive power is also situational. Two people may be negotiating about a business issue and the person with more money to spend may have more power (because that person can out-spend the other if a deal is not reached). The same two people may meet later in a dark alley where the person with less money robs the other at knife point. In the second situation, the person with the knife clearly has more power because he or she can do more if an agreement cannot be reached about how much money should be handed over to the thief.

It Happened at Mediation

A manufacturing company sued one of the purchasers of its product for breach of contract. The purchaser was a small company with few assets. It first appeared that the manufacturer had the power in the negotiation because, if a deal were not reached, it would be better able to finance the litigation and would have a strong case in court. The perception was that the manufacturer's BATNA (proceeding to court) was good and the purchaser's BATNA was not so good.

We then learned, however, that the purchaser was on the verge of bankruptcy and that the manufacturer would not recover if the matter were to go to court. The power dynamics changed since both disputants now believed that going to court would not be particularly productive for the manufacturer and not particularly bad for the purchaser.

As a result of the new power dynamics, the manufacturer agreed to settle for a fraction of the amount owing, provided it received certified cheques.

12.2   PROCESS POWER

The other kind of power in a negotiation is process power. This is the power of persuasion, the ability to negotiate effectively in any situation. Process power does not change if the facts change or if the situation changes because it is defined as the person's inherent ability to negotiate effectively.

Process power could be thought of in terms of the seven elements of principled negotiation (discussed in Chapter 3, 'Mediation: Facilitated Negotiation'). An understanding of the seven elements and an ability to use them effectively can make a person persuasive and therefore a powerful negotiator.

For example, an understanding of *alternatives* gives process power. Your alternatives are all of the things that you can do if you do not reach an agreement with the other disputant; BATNA, as previously stated, is the course of action you plan to take if no agreement is reached. Your BATNA is the best alternative that you will select from all of the possible alternatives. Alternatives give process power, not in the sense that having a better BATNA gives you substantive power, but in the sense that knowing your BATNA, knowing the consequences if you walk away from the table and knowing the consequences if the other person walks away from the table make you a more powerful negotiator.

An understanding of *interests* gives process power. Interests are the wants, needs, desires and goals behind the positions. A negotiator who understands his or her own interests, and uses a process that maximises the likelihood that those interests will be met, will be a better negotiator. A negotiator who understands that the other side's position is just their idea of how their interests might be met, and who is willing to try to uncover those hidden interests and try to accommodate them, is powerful.

An understanding of *options* gives process power. Options are the possible outcomes that you and the other negotiator can agree to in the negotiation. The effective negotiator participates in a brainstorming process to come up with as many options as possible before selecting the appropriate, durable option.

An understanding of *legitimacy* gives process power. An understanding that people are persuaded more by objective criteria than by bullying creates power since it makes a negotiator more persuasive. A powerful negotiator will also use objective criteria to assess the fairness of any offer proposed by the other person.

An understanding of *communication* gives process power. An ability to communicate effectively, both speaking and listening, translates into being a powerful negotiator. Truly effective negotiators behave as they wish others to behave. They are open to be persuaded and, as a result, others are open to be persuaded by them; they listen and, as a result, others listen to them; they talk freely about their own interests and, as a result, others talk freely about theirs.

An understanding of the relevance of *relationships* in a negotiation gives process power. Relationships play a role in almost every negotiation. Good negotiators are soft on the people and hard on the problems, dealing with people issues gently while rigorously attacking problems.

Finally, an understanding of when *commitment* is appropriate gives process power. The best negotiators commit at the end of the negotiation, not at the beginning. They don't start by committing to a position; they reach their position only after discussing interests and options with the other person and deciding which option satisfies their interests and is durable. Powerful negotiators commit to a deal only if it is better for them than their BATNA.

Process power is, then, the power to persuade and the power that goes with being an effective negotiator.

12.3   POWER IMBALANCES IN MEDIATION

When there are power imbalances, particularly extreme ones, the impact on the mediation may be significant. A person with substantive power may try to exert pressure on the weaker person, may threaten, or may try to coerce. In such a situation, the interests of the weaker person may not be met.

We should not assume that it is necessarily bad for the person with substantive power to exert that power. Sometimes people exert their power to achieve what we would believe are appropriate ends. Usually the person with the power feels justified in exercising it, and who can say that the exercise of power is not justified? If you are the person with the power in a mediation (or are representing a person with the power), you may decide that the exercise of power is appropriate and justified.

If you (or your client) are in a weaker bargaining position, you may try to lessen the substantive power imbalance. You may be concerned that the imbalance could result in a deal that is 'unfair' for you (or your client) and that the deal may be forced rather than voluntary.

When there is a substantive power imbalance, it is not the mediator's role, I believe, to correct the imbalance and 'level the playing field'. Even if the mediator believes that his or her role is to effect an objectively 'fair' result, the mediator cannot really change a power imbalance that exists, because a mediator cannot affect the disputants' BATNAs. The power imbalance exists; the disputants and their lawyers recognise it, and they have hired the mediator to help them try to settle their dispute, not take away power from one disputant and give it to the other.

It Happened at Mediation

There was a break-up of a professional practice and a dispute between the former partners about how the assets were to be divided and how the partners would deal with the ongoing files in which they were both involved. It turned out that there were a number of ongoing issues and, together, we agreed on a list. We then turned our attention to how to resolve them. One of the lawyers asked me to meet with him confidentially in private. We met and he told me that he believed I had done a good job, and that the mediation was almost over, with all of the issues resolved. Surprised, I told him that I did not understand because all that we had done was list the issues; we had not resolved them. He said that he knew that, but that he believed that his client's view on all of the issues would be accepted because the other side could not afford the cost of litigation and, more importantly, could not afford the publicity associated with the litigation. I was sceptical, but agreed to allow him the opportunity to speak first when we returned to joint session. He made his pitch and, to my surprise, the other side accepted all of his client's positions.

> He used his client's substantive power, and the fact that he and the other side both believed that the other side had a terrible BATNA (litigation) to his advantage to obtain a favourable deal for his client.

Where there is a process power imbalance and one side is more articulate and more skilled at negotiating than the other, the question of the appropriate role for the mediator to play is a more challenging one. Part of the mediator's job is to facilitate communication and help the disputants understand the interests and the options, and to compare those options with their BATNAs. Most mediators believe that it is part of their job to ensure that the process of mediation is a fair one and that each side has a fair (though not necessarily equal) opportunity to participate in the process.

The existence of a process power imbalance creates an opportunity for the powerful party to abuse the process and use it to force the other party to reach an agreement that he or she would not otherwise reach. Most mediators will attempt to ensure that the process is fair and that it is not abused in such a way that it has an inappropriate impact on the weaker disputant.

However, it is not the mediator's job to teach ineffective advocates how to become more effective.

It Happened at Mediation

Lawyers at mediation do not always have the same level of experience or skill. I was mediating one case between a young barrister who had been recently called to the Bar and an experienced barrister. The inexperienced barrister represented an individual and the experienced barrister represented a company. The individual was suing the company for the payment of money that the individual said the company owed him under a contract.

During the process of storytelling and determining interests, the experienced barrister was articulate and persuasive, while the less experienced barrister was not terribly persuasive. I tried to ensure that each side understood what the other was saying, and that the interests and issues were clear. I did not try to improve on the presentation made by the inexperienced barrister. We broke into caucus (a private meeting) and the company made an offer that the individual was going to accept, but he first asked for his lawyer's opinion of whether the offer was fair. The lawyer said that she believed so, but was not sure, so she wanted my (the mediator's) opinion of the fairness of the offer.

I felt conflicted. While I believed that the offer was probably not fair based on what I had read and heard, I did not feel that it was part of my role in this mediation to act as advisor as well as mediator and that it was inappropriate for me to comment on my views about the fairness of the offer. (To be clear, I will give my opinion on offers and arguments if both sides agree that that is part of my role, but that was not the case here.) Also, I did not know all of the motivations of both sides and I did not know the pressures that were on each disputant to settle. Finally, I could never predict what a court would do and I did not want to be responsible for suggesting that a particular offer was not fair when that offer could be better than the judgment in court.

I therefore said that it was not my role to comment on the fairness of offers, that if they wanted to adjourn the mediation to consider the offer or call someone to discuss it, those were both options available to them (in addition to the options of accepting the offer, rejecting the offer or making a counter-offer).

They accepted the offer.

12.4   THREATS OF VIOLENCE

It can happen that the substantive power imbalance creates a situation where the mediators can actually cause harm by conducting the mediation. People sometimes exercise their substantive power by becoming violent. As I have stated a number of times, my number one rule of mediation is: above all, do no harm. Where there is a threat of violence, or a potential for violence, mediators could inadvertently do something to escalate the violence. Some people exercise power by physically harming others or by threatening physical harm. My practice is to stop mediations where there is a threat of violence or potential physical harm to one of the disputants.

The danger with not terminating the mediation is that the mediator may not know the psychological effect of an outcome (or the lack of an outcome) on the disputants and cannot control how they will react.

It Happened at Mediation

I was mediating a dispute between a commercial landlord and commercial tenant regarding the alleged non-payment of rent. Both sides were represented by lawyers. During storytelling, the landlord's representative mentioned that she had been threatened by the former tenant and was fearful that one of the former tenant's 'friends' would physically harm her if she did not agree to what he was asking.

I separated the disputants into caucus and met first with the landlord's representative and her lawyer. I wanted to find out whether her comments were being put forward as a negotiation ploy or whether her fears were real. She assured me that her fears were real and I terminated the mediation.

It Happened at Mediation

A lender was suing a borrower for the non-payment of a debt and I was mediating the dispute. During the course of the mediation, I learned that the daughter of the lender used to be married to the borrower, and the ex-spouses were both present at the mediation. When we were exploring options, the borrower brainstormed the option of returning to his ex-wife to reconcile their marriage. When we began to assess options, the ex-wife suggested that that might be a good idea, but that she was fearful because the last time they were together she was beaten by her former husband.

I adjourned the mediation and referred the disputants to a different mediator who was an expert in dealing with cases of domestic violence. I understand that the disputants decided not to reconcile.

12.5   SEVERE POWER IMBALANCES

There are some who believe that society should never allow mediation to occur where a power imbalance is severe because the disempowered person will not be able to make an informed decision. The person with the power may be able to send signals to cause the disempowered person to make concessions or the disempowered person may make decisions based on fear rather than on logic.

Those who argue that these cases should not be mediated believe that the protection of the judicial system is the only way to protect the rights of the disempowered person and make sure that the result is fair.

Others argue that the court system, by its nature, favours those who have power and certainly those who have money and that it is naïve to expect the courts to protect the disempowered. They believe that it is unfair to prevent the disempowered from participating in mediation when others are free to use mediation to find solutions that are better for both sides than going to court. They believe that to deny a disempowered person the ability to choose whether or not to participate in a mediation is really, in itself, disempowering.

Those who believe mediation is appropriate in situations of extreme power imbalance, however, do believe that there are safeguards that need to be put in place to ensure a fair process and attempt to prevent an inappropriate abuse of power.

12.6   DEALING WITH POWER IMBALANCES IN MEDIATION

Where there are power imbalances, be they substantive or process-oriented, and where the mediator believes that he or she needs to take measures to ensure that the process is fair, there are a number of steps the mediator can take. If the mediator does not take any of these steps, the disputants (or their lawyers) may request that they be taken.

First, those who do not have power may require assistance at the mediation to ensure that they have an opportunity to communicate effectively and make informed decisions. The person assisting could be a lawyer, social worker, friend or relative. The disempowered person can then have the benefit of someone who can make presentations, listen and ask questions effectively. The disempowered person can also get someone who can provide relatively objective advice, assist in assessing any offer that is made and assist in formulating offers.

Mediators will often conduct a significant percentage of the mediation in caucus if the mediator believes there is a severe power imbalance. When the disputants are separate, the stronger disputant will not benefit from yelling, threatening or otherwise abusing a power imbalance. If the mediator knows ahead of time that there may be a severe power imbalance at the mediation, he or she may decide to conduct the entire mediation in private session and prevent any direct contact between the disputants.

If the disputants are in the joint session, the mediator will strictly enforce ground rules. For example, the mediator will ensure that no one is interrupted.

To be clear, however, not all mediators believe it is appropriate to do anything when there is a power imbalance, no matter how severe, as they do not believe it is the mediator's role to balance power. They conduct the mediation as they would any other mediation, keeping in mind, however, that if there is a threat or fear of violence, the mediator may terminate the process.

Tips for Lawyers

- Sometimes in mediation you have power, and sometimes you lack it. If you have substantive power, you need not hide the fact that it is important for the other side to reach a deal and that your client has a strong BATNA. At the same time, threats or yelling can destroy otherwise productive discussions. You will still need to focus on trying to help your client get a deal that is better than his or her BATNA.

- If your client does not have substantive power compared to the other disputant, you will want to refer to objective criteria in order to encourage the other side to do what is fair. You will want to stay away from discussions about the consequences of not reaching agreement.

- Regardless of the substantive power in the mediation, you can improve your process power by becoming a more skilled negotiator and using the seven elements of principled negotiation.

Tips for Mediators

- It is not your job to balance substantive power imbalances; they exist in mediations and the mediator is not hired to balance power. You can and should, however, try to make the process fair and give everyone an opportunity to speak and participate effectively in the process.

- If you are concerned that there is a severe power imbalance and that you may not be able to facilitate the discussion so as to provide everyone with an opportunity to speak and consider issues raised, you may choose to conduct the entire mediation through caucuses. You may also want to ensure that participants are represented by those who can give them advice and assistance.

- If there is an extreme power imbalance and you fear that the mediation may result in physical harm to one of the disputants, you should terminate the mediation.

CHAPTER 13

POSITIONAL BARGAINING

13.1 PEOPLE GET STUCK ON POSITIONS

The most common version of 'hitting the wall' (see the discussion in Chapter 11, 'Overcoming Obstacles') is having the disputants get stuck on positions, anchor and not be prepared to consider other options or make further compromises. What can a mediator do to refocus people away from their positions, into a problem-solving mode that is more likely to reach a resolution?

A common reason for anchoring is that people believe that they will win if they go to trial. They have looked at the facts as they know them, applied the law as they understand it and concluded that they have a strong case. Often, as I stated earlier, both sides believe that they have a strong case, that they will win if the issue goes to trial, and that if the other side really understood how strong their case was, the other side would make a more reasonable offer.

At least one of the sides that does this analysis is wrong. Even the best lawyers have a tendency to overvalue their cases (though almost all lawyers believe that they are the exception to the rule and can objectively assess their cases). When lawyers assess the likely outcome of a dispute, they have heard everything from their own client's perspective and not from the other side. Also, they have looked at the law with a view to how it could be used to win their case, not how it could be used to defeat it. This is not a criticism of lawyers; it is a reality of the litigation process. The challenge is how to overcome the obstacle.

People take positions for a number of reasons. Often, they take positions because they believe what they are saying is fair and reasonable. Sometimes they take positions that they know to be unfair or unreasonable, believing that if they take a position and stick to it, the other side will capitulate or at least make concessions that they would not otherwise have made.

There are a number of things that disputants, lawyers and mediators can do when the other disputant takes a position and anchors.

13.1.1 Look at Best Alternatives to a Negotiated Agreement (BATNAs)

Disputants often believe that their primary task in assessing an offer from the other side is examining the reasonableness of the offer. They assess the offer according to their perception of its fairness because they believe that is the correct test to apply. Unfortunately, that is not the correct test. The proper test is whether what is proposed is better or worse than not settling. Everyone would prefer to trade a deal that is not reasonable for a deal that is reasonable. Often, however, disputants are rejecting a deal that is unreasonable and are left with no deal at all. They are forced to proceed with their BATNA, which may not strike them as fair or reasonable either.

It is the job of the lawyer and the mediator to discuss (in caucus) with the disputants the consequences of not reaching an agreement. In order to make informed decisions, disputants need to know the facts and risks associated with their

BATNA, which is often going to trial. If their BATNA is litigation, each disputant will need to be aware of the cost of continuing with the litigation, the likelihood of losing, the time and effort that will be expended and the emotional drain of litigation. They will also need to be reminded of the unpredictability of litigation, even if they are right and the other side lies.

Talking with disputants about their BATNA is a powerful way to help disputants rethink their insistence on sticking to positions, even if they believe the positions to be fair. Mediators will usually wait until the mediation has reached the wall before talking about the BATNA.

Sometimes people consider that their BATNA is not settling now, but settling later. They do not want to settle because they assume that the last offer that was made will always be there for them if they want it. Sometimes that is true; at other times it is not.

It Happened at Mediation

A group of companies and consumer groups were meeting to discuss whether they could agree on a process for pricing certain products that would be fair to consumer groups and produce a fair return for the companies. If they could reach a unanimous consensus, they could recommend the outcome to the government regulatory agency, which had indicated that it would probably accept any unanimous recommendation. The discussions were complex and the initial meetings lasted for five days. At the end of the five days, the consumer groups and some of the companies had an approach that they thought was workable, but some of the other companies were not persuaded. These other groups believed that, if they adjourned, the consumer groups would feel pressure and would agree to something more favourable to the companies.

Unfortunately for the companies, the opposite occurred. During the break, the consumer groups became more entrenched and were not prepared to agree to what had been proposed at the first session. The groups were unable to reach a consensus.

If a disputant wants to reject an offer because he or she assumes it will always be on the table, the mediator may speak to the disputant about the dangers in making that assumption.

13.1.2 Talk about interests, not positions

The results at trial may not be ideal. Disputants want what is best for them, and that is not always what a court can or would award. It is the job of lawyers and mediators to help the disputants focus on whether their interests are better met by pursuing litigation (even if they win) or by coming up with a creative settlement that satisfies their interests.

13.1.3 Go back in the process

One technique to help deal with a positional bargainer is to go back to other stages in the mediation process to see what may have been missed. This may involve, for example, referring back to the interests that were established and having disputants refocus on their interests rather than their positions. Interests can sometimes emerge late in the mediation process.

Disputants may be stuck on their positions because there is an information gap. They may need more information from the other side in order to be able to expand the pie and come up with creative options. To test this hypothesis, the mediator may return to the storytelling stage and ask the disputants to talk more about what has upset them and what the problem is from their perspective.

It Happened at Mediation

The issue in a mediation was the appropriate rent that was to be paid by a group of tenants to a landlord relating to a cottage development. We were examining some of the options presented and were in a shuttle diplomacy stage. I was presenting an offer to the tenants from the landlord based on rent that was paid by cottage owners in another district, and the tenant group told me that the offer was completely unacceptable. Rather than ask for a counter-offer, I explored with the tenants why the offer was not fair based on the objective criteria that we had. The tenant group said that the inhabitants in the other district had their grass cut twice a week (instead of once), had burned-out light bulbs replaced in 24 hours (instead of 48 hours), and had telephone calls to the landlord returned immediately (instead of waiting a couple of days).

It was clear that there were interests that had not yet emerged that needed to be met if options were to be accepted. I told the landlord of the interests and the landlord was happy to set up a process to address them. This made the process of coming up with a fair price easy.

13.1.4 Build on what disputants agree on

When referring back to earlier parts of the mediation, the mediator will try to help the disputants recall the successes they have had thus far in the process, and build on the progress they have made. If they have understood each other's interests, listened to each other and recognised that the process is a contest of the disputants against a problem rather than the disputants against each other, they can build on the successes and use them to help resolve their issues. If some issues have been resolved (even minor ones), the disputants can see that they can solve problems and resolve conflict between them. If they feel that they can work together effectively, they are more likely to find a way to solve the more difficult issues.

It Happened at Mediation

I was mediating a dispute between a bank and a number of employees. The employees were complaining about working conditions at the bank and were asking for damages for their suffering as a result of unsafe working conditions. The employees were still working for the bank and believed that the problem (unsafe working conditions) had been corrected.

The bank recognised that the working conditions had been unsafe but stated that under no circumstances could they compensate the employees. Their underlying interest was that the precedent was unpalatable as other bank employees may also ask for money from the bank. This was a situation where the relationship was clearly ongoing, the employees were valued employees, and yet the bank steadfastly refused to compensate them.

I continued to focus the discussion on the positive aspects of the relationship, and what the bank was doing for the employees. I learned in the course of the discussion that the bank supported an employee charity initiative, in which the employees were helping design a park in a low-income part of town. The creative solution that the disputants came up with was that the bank would put more money into the charitable project and the employees could use the money to build extra facilities on the playground. The bank's interests were met because it did not have to take money from its compensation budget, and the employees felt vindicated. Their interest in personal recognition was met by the bank agreeing to post a plaque at the playground thanking the employees (who had worked in unsafe conditions) for their contribution to the park.

Mediators will struggle to find any common ground or agreement between disputants, even if it is not substantive and even if it is at the mediator's expense. For example, I have had situations where both disputants agreed that I was dragging out the process, that it was taking too long or that I (as mediator) was not focused enough on the issues. They expressed their frustration with me. While it was a bit tough on my ego, I used the fact that they were upset with me to show them that there were things they agreed on (that they were upset with me) and they were not at odds about everything.

13.1.5 Take a break

An obvious (and yet often forgotten) option for dealing with a positional bargainer is to take a break. Sometimes, tensions rise and disputants are not able to focus clearly on solving the problem. A break can refocus them on what is really important.

It Happened at Mediation

I was mediating a dispute relating to the break-up of a couple and, while most of the financial issues between the former spouses had been sorted out, they were unable to agree on how to divide some relatively insignificant assets. When tensions rose and the disputants started engaging in personal attacks, I decided it would be a good time for a break. I asked them to focus during the break on the effect of the conflict on their daughter. When we returned, the atmosphere was completely different. The husband had drafted a proposed schedule for the division of the assets based on the requests of the wife, and the mediation concluded relatively quickly and with minimal acrimony. The husband said that once he thought about the impact of the fight on their daughter, he saw that it was not worth it to fight over insignificant assets.

Disputants can lose sight of the fact that they have an ongoing relationship. People sometimes focus on the substance of the dispute and forget that they must live together in this very small world.

It is not unusual during a dispute for people to believe that they have absolutely nothing in common with the other side and that they cannot agree on anything. During a break, they may discuss issues not relating to the mediation and may find that they do, indeed, have things in common.

It Happened at Mediation

A number of years ago, I was acting as a lawyer in a dispute that was well into the litigation process. I believed that the other lawyer was completely unreasonable, unco-operative and incapable of even considering valid settlement options. The mediation was particularly acrimonious and was leading nowhere when the mediator suggested that we take a break and grab a coffee at the coffee shop. It was a conscious decision, I believe, to get us out of our environment of conflict.

While we were having coffee, the other lawyer saw a newspaper and commented that he was frustrated that his favourite hockey team, the Toronto Maple Leafs, was doing so poorly. Now, the Maple Leafs are my favourite team as well. I found myself being angry that he had the same favourite team as I. After all, he was unreasonable, unco-operative, and (I believed) a bad person. How could he cheer for my team?

Of course, my reaction was illogical, and I started thinking about why I reacted as I did. I realised that my mindset was so focused on the fact that the other lawyer was evil, that I could not focus objectively on the issue that we needed to resolve. I had blinkers on and I had to open my mind and try to listen better. If this were my reaction to his comment about his favourite hockey team, I must also be reacting negatively to his suggestions about settlement and not seriously considering them.

13.1.6 Explore unwanted options

One of my favourite techniques for dealing with positional bargainers is to ask them to assume that a judge or some higher authority orders them to accept the offer that the other side is proposing and to go down the path that they do not want to go down. If that were the case, what would have to happen for the situation to be palatable? Disputants are usually reluctant to explore paths they don't like. When they do, however, they sometimes find that their interests can be addressed by proceeding down the other path with some creative thinking.

It Happened at Mediation

I was mediating a dispute among a board of directors about whether the company should merge with another company. Half of the board thought that the merger was absolutely necessary for the survival of the company and the other half thought that a merger would be disastrous and that all that the company had worked for would be lost. I asked those who were in favour of the merger to tell me what they would like to see happen if there could be no merger, and I asked the other group (that opposed the merger) to tell me how the merged entity would have to be structured for it to meet the group's interests. Needless to say, both sides were initially reluctant. I told them to assume that they had no choice about whether a merger would occur – if they wanted a merger it would not occur and if they did not want a merger it would occur. They, however, could define the terms.

The group that was opposed to the merger then came up with a corporate structure that maintained the name of the company, provided for a minimum number of directors from their company on the new board, and prevented the new company from acting in contravention of the moral and ethical approach that the current company was currently adopting. The group discovered that those who favoured the merger were in agreement with those principles, and the merger discussions went ahead with the unanimous support of the board.

It Happened at Mediation

I discussed earlier a mediation between a commercial landlord and commercial tenant concerning who should be required to pay for leasehold improvements. The tenant was withholding rent and the landlord refused to participate in the mediation unless the rent was paid up to date.

To try to bring the disputants together, I asked the landlord to think about what would have to happen for him to participate without receiving rent cheques, and I asked the tenant under what circumstances would he pay the rent arrears before the mediation. It was in the context of that discussion that the tenant said that if he got a letter from the landlord that could help him with respect to his relationship with his bank, he would agree to pay the rent arrears and participate in the mediation. The landlord agreed, the mediation continued and, as you may recall, the disputants ended up taking a trip to Las Vegas together.

13.1.7 Doing what comes naturally

Sometimes we just have to trust our instincts and do what comes naturally. Remember that rule number two of mediation is that, other than making sure that no one leaves the mediation in a worse position than when they arrived, there are no absolute rules. If all else seems to fail, do what comes naturally.

It Happened at Mediation

A colleague of mine was mediating the break-up between two partners of a small business. Throughout the process, they maintained a positional approach and would not compromise or discuss creative options. They refused to brainstorm. The mediator found it difficult to maintain his composure and, after a few hours, he eventually cracked. He expressed his frustration and anger to the disputants,

> telling them that they were both being obstructionist, uncreative and difficult. He told them that he was finished with the mediation, that they deserved each other and he wished them luck in court. He then went over to the window to calm down.
>
> While he was there, a strange thing happened. One of the disputants said, 'You know, he's right. We have been difficult'. The other one said, 'Maybe we should try some of that brainstorming he was telling us to try', and the disputants started brainstorming options.
>
> The mediator listened silently at the window. After all, yelling at the disputants was the first technique he had used all day that had succeeded. Eventually one of the disputants called to him and said, 'Are you going to look out the window all day or are you going to come over here and help us?'

This is not to suggest that it is a good idea for a mediator to shout at the disputants; it is the rare case where shouting will achieve its objective. However, expressing true feelings and doing what comes naturally can sometimes work where other more proven techniques do not.

13.1.8 The double blind

When it appears that the mediation is over because one or both of the disputants have taken positions, are not prepared to make compromises from the positions or are unable to come up with a deal and are arguing about money, it's time for the double blind. The double blind is a somewhat controversial technique used by some mediators to try to bridge the gap between two positions at the end of the mediation.

The double blind works as follows. The mediator takes some time to think about all that has been said in the mediation (in joint session and caucus (private session)) and comes up with what the mediator believes is a fair resolution to the dispute (often a number in between the two positions that are being maintained). The mediator meets with the disputants and their lawyers in private session and presents the mediator's proposed solution to the disputants. There is no discussion, argument or debate about the proposal. The mediator presents the same proposed solution to each side (though does not necessarily say the same speech to each side about why the deal is fair and makes sense for them).

The disputants and their lawyers then meet without the mediator to discuss the mediator's proposal and decide whether it is acceptable in its entirety. Each side can choose either to accept or to reject the mediator's proposal. The mediator then returns to each caucus room and learns, in confidence from each disputant, whether that disputant would be prepared to accept the deal if the other disputant accepted as well. If both sides accept, there is a deal. If either rejects, there is not a deal and the mediation is over (unless both of the disputants want to continue discussions).

The magic of the double blind is that each side is only entitled to hear whether the other side would accept or reject the proposal if and when that side accepts and is prepared to commit to the proposal. If a disputant does not accept the proposal, that disputant does not learn whether the other side said yes or no.

There is therefore no risk to participating in the double blind for either side. If a disputant says yes, that disputant is only committing to a solution provided the other side simultaneously accepts the proposal. If the disputant says no, nothing is lost. There is no danger that one side will say yes and the other will say no and that the person who said yes will be at a disadvantage by having compromised from his or her initial position.

While it is tempting, the objective for the mediator is not to split the difference between the two positions (although that may sometimes be the fair solution). The mediator should choose a solution that is fair. However, the mediator will have to deal with the disputants' expectation that what will be proposed will not be worse than splitting the difference.

The dangers of the double blind are similar to the dangers of the one text. Both processes put a lot of power in the hands of the mediator. For a double blind, the mediator chooses the solution that the two sides are asked to accept and there will necessarily be some subjectivity in the assessment. Mediators necessarily lose some of their neutrality in the process, and that is why it can only be done at the end of the mediation, after all other techniques have been attempted.

All in all, though, a double blind can be an effective way of overcoming a situation where disputants have entrenched positions. In my experience, far more often than not, the disputants agree with what the mediator proposes. It is a way of allowing them to save face and avoid trial.

It Happened at Mediation

In a dispute about the amount of money owing for a breach of contract, the disputants initially disagreed about whether any money was owing and, if money was owing, how much. After a lot of discussion and exploration of creative payment terms, the claimant still demanded £100,000 and the defendant was only prepared to pay £80,000. It was clear to both disputants that the cost of going to trial would be far greater than the £20,000 difference and that they each risked significantly worse result than either £80,000 or £100,000. All of that being said, they were both prepared to walk out.

I proposed a double blind and both sides accepted. I considered the situation and concluded (and told both sides) that I believed a fair solution was payment of £92,000 over a period of time. My conclusion was based on the fact that there had been some discussions about potential damages when the contract was entered into, and the discussion had been centred on £92,000.

The claimant reluctantly accepted the £92,000, though he was upset that the payment was over time. The defendant, though, was extremely upset that I had not split the difference between the two positions, and initially refused to accept. I spent some time with the defendant explaining the reasons why I thought the fair number was not a split of the difference. The defendant asked me to reconsider, and I said that I could not, as the rules were that I was to choose a solution and that there was to be no negotiation. After a time, the defendant agreed to pay £92,000, preferring that to going to court.

Once both sides had accepted, I was able to tell both of them that they had a deal.

Tips for Lawyers

- Your client may become positional, focused on winning and the perceived 'matter of principle', rather than what may be in the client's best interest. Clients have a right to fight about principle; the lawyer's job is to make sure that the client is making an informed decision. If you, as the lawyer, believe that your client is turning down a deal that he or she should accept, you will need to discuss your concerns with your client. Clients have the right to make the final decision, of course, but they usually want the input that you can provide based on your experience.

- Discussion does not mean merely telling your client what to do. Your clients will first need to hear from you that you understand their dilemma and position. Your clients need to feel that you are on their side. Only then may your clients be open to your concerns and suggestions. The key, then, is first to repeat your clients' arguments back to them in the best possible light (interactively listen), and then to present your views on what your clients have decided.

- If the other side is being positional and does not appear open to your ideas (even if you believe your ideas are fair), there are a number of techniques you may want to employ. You will first and foremost want to show that you are open to be persuaded, using the behaviour that you want the other side to adopt. You may want to explore with the other side (or ask the mediator to explore) their BATNA. You may want to focus on the parts of the dispute that you and the other side agree on, trying to build on the successes that you have achieved. You may need a break, even for a day or two.

- At the end of the mediation, you may want to leave an offer with the other disputant open for a period of time. After reflection, the other disputant may reconsider your offer or may ask for further meetings to discuss options.

Tips for Mediators

- When disputants get positional, you may want to meet with them in private to talk to them about their BATNAs and the danger of not settling. You may also want to talk about their interests and how those interests can be met in the future either through continuing with the litigation process or by settling. Try to pick your time to talk about BATNAs, as this tool should not be used too early. You should wait until you have 'hit the wall'.

- Be careful not to embarrass lawyers in front of their clients, or one side in front of the other. If a lawyer says something that you believe is completely wrong (and the lawyer should know what is right), ask for a caucus with the lawyer to discuss the issue.

- If disputants are stuck on one issue but have reached agreement on other issues, you may want to return to the issues on which they have agreed to remind them of their successes. The refocus can sometimes create breakthroughs for the disputants. You may also consider using a 'one text'.

- When disputants are stuck, proceeding down two separate paths that will probably never meet, you may want to ask them to assume that they have to agree to what the other side insists upon, and ask them to create a scenario where that path could lead to a resolution that would be palatable.

- There is nothing wrong with taking a break. As long as the antagonism between the disputants is not too great, you may want them to break in the same room. Difficult obstacles can often be overcome during social discussions over coffee.

- A double blind is a last resort, when all other attempts to have disputants agree have failed. Before commencing with the double blind, you will want to speak with each disputant separately (each with their lawyer) and express to them their arguments at their strongest. If they feel that you understand their arguments, they are more likely to accept your proposal.

- When presenting the double blind proposal, do not engage in discussion with either side about how the proposal could be amended; the identical proposal must be made to both sides.

CHAPTER 14

CLOSURE

There are three possibilities at the end of the mediation: the disputants do not reach an agreement; the disputants reach a partial agreement; or the disputants reach a full agreement. In each situation, what should the mediator do? Should the mediation necessarily end when the disputants reach agreement? How do disputants know that they cannot make the agreement better? If there is a final agreement, who should draft it? Should it be drafted in the room at the end of the mediation or at a later time? How can disputants make sure that the agreement will be adhered to? Should the agreement remain confidential?

14.1   NO AGREEMENT OR PARTIAL AGREEMENT

When disputants reach an agreement, it is clear that the mediation is over. It is sometimes difficult to know when a mediation should stop in situations where no agreement has been reached. Mediators and disputants do not want to stop before all reasonable avenues for settlement have been explored. The mediation is clearly over if one side walks out. The mediation is also over when the mediator has conducted a double blind and one of the disputants has not agreed to the mediator's proposed solution. Otherwise, the clearest signal that it is time to end the mediation is that both (or all) disputants believe that there is nothing else they can do, and the mediator has no other ideas.

When the mediation ends with no agreement, the mediator will probably first attempt to determine whether there are any issues on which the disputants do agree. If there has been some agreement, a document should be drafted (as discussed below) setting out what has been agreed. For issues that are not resolved, the mediator will work with the disputants to help them clarify the issues and agree on the process steps to bring the issues to resolution. For example, the disputants may decide to go to arbitration, or may decide to continue with litigation and set a schedule for exchange of documents.

Even where the disputants have not agreed on any of the issues, the mediator may help the disputants see what progress has been made in the mediation, in the hope that, at some future time, the disputants will focus on the progress and perhaps resolve the dispute. They may even agree to meet again, either with or without the mediator.

Finally, the mediator will thank the disputants for their participation in the mediation process and end the mediation.

14.2   COMPLETE SETTLEMENT

The disputants may reach agreement while in joint session or while in caucus (where an offer presented by one disputant, through the mediator, is accepted by the other). Once an agreement has been reached, the disputants and the mediator should first make sure that there has, in fact, been agreement on all of the issues. Sometimes disputants focus on the most contentious issue, resolve it and believe that the mediation is over. Of course, all issues must be resolved before the mediation is over.

Once it is clear that all issues have been resolved, the mediator will probably confirm (orally) with each of the disputants the precise terms of the agreement, and reconfirm that the disputants at the table have the authority to agree to the settlement.

It Happened at Mediation

I was mediating a dispute between a council and members of a family who had been injured after slipping on an icy walkway. The family was suing the council for negligence. In the settlement discussions, it became apparent that it was important to one of the injured children to receive a letter from the council apologising for the injuries. The council's representative heard the interest and proposed that the council write a letter to the young child apologising. An agreement was eventually reached on the other issues. In the discussion that followed confirming authority, the council's representative mentioned that she herself did not have the authority to commit to the letter, only to recommend it. She did have the authority to commit to the financial and other aspects of the agreement. The written agreement therefore had to be drafted so as not to require the letter, but rather to indicate that a request for the letter would be made and that a letter would probably be forthcoming.

Some agreements result in the disputants having an ongoing relationship while others do not. Where there will be an ongoing relationship, the disputants may want to consider how to resolve disputes that might arise, either as a result of the implementation of the agreement or in future negotiations. For complex mediations in particular, the disputants may be concerned that they will have to address unanticipated issues when they attempt to implement the agreement. Even for simple mediations, issues can arise relating to, for example, the drafting of the release.

If the disputants were pleased with the mediation process, they may want to agree to return to mediation if they have another dispute. They may decide that any dispute will be resolved through an inexpensive and simple arbitration process (perhaps even where everyone agrees that the mediator would act as the arbitrator).

Regardless of whether the relationship is ongoing, one issue that the disputants may want to consider is how they will deal with a breach of the settlement agreement. An agreement reached at mediation has the same legal effect as an agreement reached privately by the disputants, and it could be breached. There are a number of options for enforcement. It may be that the agreement can be filed with the court on consent (if the dispute is within the context of litigation) and one of the disputants can seek a consent order that the settlement is enforceable as a judgment of the court. It may be that one disputant gives the other a consent to judgment if certain conditions are not fulfilled. For example, one side may be required to make payments over time and the disputant agreeing to make payments may agree that, if he or she misses a payment, the other disputant can go to court and obtain judgment for the balance owing. It may be that the disputants agree to binding arbitration in case of an alleged breach of the agreement (perhaps preceded by a return to mediation) or it may be that enforcement is not an issue. Regardless, the disputants and their lawyers should consider the issue of enforcement.

14.3   *PARETO* OPTIMALITY

Most of us make the assumption that, once a deal is reached, we have finished with the negotiation and it would be a waste of time to continue the negotiation. After all, we have reached a deal. But how do we know that the first deal that we have reached is the best deal? When we negotiate, we do not always disclose all information and we may posture. While that can, on occasion, help us achieve a better deal, it may also prevent us from exploring options. Sometimes, despite the best efforts of the mediator, disputants are not willing to disclose everything and explore all possible options, and yet they reach agreement.

Once the deal is reached, however, it may make sense for the disputants to explore whether there are ways to improve it. What about the danger that, after a discussion, one of the disputants will not be prepared to accept even the initial deal? One way to deal with this concern is to explore options on the clear understanding that, if the initial deal cannot be improved upon (or if any improvement for one disputant results in a worse deal for the other), both sides will be bound by the initial deal. Once they have a deal and agree that they are both bound by their agreement to honour it, they can benefit from exploring whether they can make the deal even better. The exercise of searching for the best deal is what is known in economics as searching for the *Pareto* optimal solution. A *Pareto* optimal solution is one that cannot be made better for one side without being made worse for the other.

Once a deal is reached, it is often worthwhile for the disputants to spend even five or ten minutes trying to determine whether there are ways that they can revise and improve the agreement they have just reached.

It Happened at Mediation

I was mediating a dispute between a member of a self-governing profession and the governing body (the College). The College alleged that the member treated a patient with disrespect and acted in an inappropriate manner. Throughout the mediation, the member (who was in his late 60s) complained about the process the College had subjected him to, and alleged that his rights had been violated. The College insisted that the public had to be protected by having him punished.

In order to avoid the cost and humiliation of a hearing, the member agreed to accept a suspension of his licence for one year. We were in the process of drafting the agreement and we decided to spend a few minutes in case we could come up with a *Pareto* superior deal. We knew that, if we could not, we would go forward with the one-year suspension.

We then started discussing the fact that the member was over retirement age and wanted to retire. He felt that he could not, however, because he had to be a mentor to his successor so that she could get her licence. (A person in that profession had to have had a mentor for a period of years before applying for a licence.)

We then discussed the possibility of the member retiring and having the student's mentor be another member of the profession. That resolution appeared to be *Pareto* superior to the one we had previously reached.

We then learned that the student had been working for many years (though she had not officially had a mentor) and probably had the skills to practise on her own.

The people at the mediation decided that they could make the deal even better by giving the student a test and, if she received higher than a certain grade, she could receive her licence without the mentoring requirement. (The mentoring requirement had been waived for others who had significant experience.) All of those present at the mediation (including the student) believed that this deal was much better than a one-year suspension for the member. The member resigned with dignity and the student got her licence. The disputants had changed their agreement to a *Pareto* superior deal.

14.4   CONFIDENTIALITY OF THE AGREEMENT

As was stated in Chapter 2, 'Why Mediate?', most mediations are confidential processes. If agreement is reached, however, does it always make sense for the agreement to be confidential? That is for the disputants to decide. Sometimes, one or both disputants will be concerned about the consequences if some of the information in the settlement agreement is made public. For example, an employer settling a wrongful dismissal case where other former employees are also suing for wrongful dismissal will probably insist that the terms of any settlement be confidential. On the other hand, it may be that the disputants, as part of the settlement discussions, determine that they want some or all of the terms of the settlement to be public.

It Happened At Mediation

A child was on a class field trip and was seriously injured. The injured student and the family sued the group that took the class on the trip. Part of the settlement at the mediation was that rules were to be implemented for all future class trips. It was important to the family that it be made public that the reason for the rules was the accident that had occurred on the ill-fated field trip, and one of the terms of the settlement was that it be made public that the new rules arose as part of the settlement of the dispute.

14.5   WHO SHOULD DRAFT SETTLEMENT DOCUMENTS?

Any agreement that is reached will have to be put in writing. Mediators should avoid drafting agreements at mediations. There are a number of dangers inherent in mediators doing the drafting. If the mediator is not a lawyer, it could be argued that the drafting is the unauthorised practice of law. If the mediator is a lawyer, it could be argued that, by doing the drafting, the mediator is practising law, is acting for both sides and therefore has disclosure obligations (so, for example, the mediator cannot keep information confidential that the mediator received from one side in confidence). Further, if an issue arises at a later time about the interpretation of words in the agreement, the drafter may be called upon to interpret the words and the mediator who drafted it may find himself or herself in the middle of a lawsuit.

That is not to say that the mediator should not be a scribe if the lawyers or the disputants dictate; it is only to say that there are dangers to the mediator actually drafting what he or she believes has been agreed. Also, the mediator may want to participate in the discussion about language if an issue arises or is inadvertently missed.

If the agreement is simple, the lawyers can sometimes write up the entire agreement at the mediation session. Once it is written, it can be dated and signed by the disputants.

More commonly, however, the terms of the agreement that is reached will not be able to be completely set out at the mediation. The final agreement will often require 'boilerplate' language that the disputants do not have at the mediation. In those cases, the lawyers should produce at the mediation minutes of settlement based on the terms that have been agreed at the mediation. Those minutes of settlement can be signed and the lawyers can then go to their offices and draft the final agreement over a number of days.

Often, releases or mutual releases will need to be exchanged. Releases state that the disputants agree that the settlement ends the dispute and the disputants release each other from claims that may exist against each other at the time. The minutes of settlement will often state that releases are to be drafted and signed over the next few days. The actual drafting of the releases will occur at the lawyers' offices.

Where disputants are not represented by lawyers at mediation, they will sometimes reach a tentative agreement and adjourn the mediation so that they can get legal advice. At other times, they will sign settlement documents at the mediation.

It is not unusual for there to be a dispute that arises during the drafting of the minutes of settlement.

It Happened at Mediation

I was mediating a breach of contract dispute and the settlement involved the payment of a substantial sum of money. While the amount was agreed, it became clear during the drafting that the terms for payment (such as the timing) were not agreed. I therefore had to mediate this issue as I would any other, determining interests, brainstorming options and applying objective criteria.

This case settled, as do the vast majority when issues occur during the drafting. At that late point in the mediation, the disputants and lawyers are tired, and the relationship between disputants has often improved. Compromises are more forthcoming.

After the minutes of settlement are drafted, the disputants will need to consider whether there are any formal reporting requirements. Do either the disputants, the mediator, or both have to report to a court? Does a formal report need to be produced? Is there a governing body or administrative agency that requires notice of the result of the mediation?

Tips for Lawyers

- If a deal is reached at mediation, take the time to write down what has been agreed. At the end of the mediation, people are tired and often do not want to deal with mundane issues (such as drafting). It is far preferable to draft a summary of what has been agreed to at the mediation (and have the disputants sign that they agree) rather than wait until later. If issues arise, the mediator will be there to address them. Also, people's memories are fresh and they can all recall what was agreed; the next day, people may have different recollections.

- It will be the lawyers' task to draft the terms of the agreement at the mediation, not the mediator's. If you anticipate that there is 'boilerplate' language that you may need, it may be helpful to bring it with you to the mediation.

- The minutes of settlement will have to address not only the substantive issues in dispute, but also the issue of releases and, in the context of litigation, how the action will be dismissed, who will do the dismissal and who will pay the fees.

- If the mediation does not result in a settlement, and your client has made a settlement offer in the mediation that was not accepted, you may want to consider making the offer formally outside the mediation.

Tips for Mediators

- Once the disputants reach an agreement, you may want to consider asking them to spend five or ten minutes to see if they can make the agreement any better. If they are reluctant, this is probably not something you should insist on.

- Mediators should avoid drafting agreements at mediations. It should be left to the disputants and their lawyers to write down what has been agreed. The mediator can assist and give guidance, and can even be a scribe, but should not do the actual drafting.

- A mediator may be mediating a case in which lawyers are not present to draft the agreement. In those situations, there are a number of options: the disputants can draft their agreement to be conditional on the approval of each side's lawyer; the mediation could adjourn so that the disputants can sit with lawyers to draft an agreement (and the mediation can resume if there are any issues that arise in the drafting of the agreement); or the disputants can agree that they will draft without lawyers.

CHAPTER 15

CONCLUSION

Disputes often involve complex issues and acrimony. They also often occur between disputants who have an ongoing relationship. Mediation provides the disputants with an opportunity to resolve their dispute quickly and inexpensively, in a way that maintains (if not improves) their relationship. It also provides a structure that allows them to explore creative options and overcome seemingly insurmountable obstacles.

There is no one right structure for mediation. Mediators have different styles and approaches. The most effective mediators adapt their approach to the type of dispute and the disputants, and use the approach that maximises the likelihood that an agreement will be reached.

Mediation is not meant to resolve all disputes and it should not be considered a failure if the mediation does not result in settlement. Some disputes need to be resolved in court or through arbitration. Mediation does create an opportunity to explore whether settlement makes sense for both disputants and, if so, facilitates the disputants' abilities to work toward that settlement.

I have tried in this book to set out one model of mediation that I believe is a good approach for mediating disputes. I have tried to provide advice and tips for both lawyers and mediators to help them navigate the mediation waters and overcome some of the common obstacles that occur in mediation.

The mediation process, however, is a fluid one, and people do not always act in a predictable way. I learn from every mediation, gathering new tools and new techniques to use in future mediations. As soon as I finish a mediation, I sit down and make notes of the things that I think I did effectively and the difficulties I encountered. I then try to think of ways that I may approach those difficulties if they arise in future mediations. This self-analysis helps me learn from my experiences.

My hope in writing this book is to give you the benefit of some of my experiences (successes and failures) so that you can participate more effectively in mediations and learn from your experiences.

I welcome your comments about the book or about mediation in general. Please feel free to e-mail me at allan@adr.ca.

APPENDIX A

SAMPLE AGREEMENT TO MEDIATE AND TERMS OF MEDIATION

1   THE PROCESS

The parties agree to attempt to settle their dispute through the mediation process on the terms contained in this agreement.

2   PARTY CONFIDENTIALITY

The parties acknowledge and agree that mediation is a confidential settlement process, and is without prejudice.

3   MEDIATOR CONFIDENTIALITY

The mediator will not disclose to anyone who is not a party to the mediation anything said in the mediation or any materials submitted to the mediator, except:

(a) to the lawyers or other professionals retained on behalf of the parties, as deemed appropriate or necessary by the mediator;

(b) to any other individual providing the parties have given written consent;

(c) for research or education purposes on an anonymous basis;

(d) where ordered to do so by a judicial authority or where required to do so by law; or

(e) where the information suggests that there will be an actual or potential threat to human life or safety, or the commission of a crime in the future.

4   IDENTITY OF MEDIATOR

The mediator is [*name of mediator*].

5   MEDIATOR AS A WITNESS

At no time will any party call the mediator as a witness to testify as to the fact of the mediation or as to any oral or written communication made at any stage of the mediation. No party will seek access to any documents prepared for or in connection with the mediation, including, but not limited to, any records, notes or work product of the mediator other than this agreement to mediate. Any party or the mediator may produce and rely upon the agreement to mediate as proof of the terms and conditions by which the mediation was governed.

6   MEDIATOR'S ROLE

The mediator's role is to assist the parties to negotiate. The mediator will not make decisions for the parties about how the matter should or must be resolved.

7   PRE-MEDIATION INFORMATION

To facilitate an understanding of the controversy and the issues to be mediated, the parties will provide the mediator with a brief written summary (to a maximum of 10 pages) of the controversy as they see it, not less than four days prior to the first mediation session.

8   AUTHORITY TO SETTLE

The parties or those representing them at the mediation will have full, unqualified authority to settle the controversy.

9   PARTIES' OWN LAWYERS

The parties agree that they may seek legal representation or advice prior to or during the mediation. They may have lawyers present at the mediation if they so desire. Although the mediator is a qualified lawyer he or she will not provide legal representation or legal advice to any party at any time, and has no duty to assert or protect the legal rights and responsibilities of any party, to raise any issue not raised by the parties themselves, or to determine who should participate in the mediation.

10   RIGHT TO WITHDRAW

Each party's participation in the mediation is voluntary. While each party intends to participate in the mediation to attempt to reach settlement, any party or the mediator may withdraw from the mediation at any time for any reason. The mediator may also terminate the mediation.

11   MEDIATION SESSIONS

The scheduled mediation session will be on [date] at [time].

12   COSTS OF THE MEDIATOR

The cost of the mediation is £ [cost] for one day of mediation (including preparation time) [or per hour], plus expenses [and taxes, if any].

13   CONSENT TO THIS AGREEMENT

Each of us has read this agreement and agrees to proceed with the mediation on the terms contained herein.

This agreement may be executed in counterparts. Execution and delivery of a facsimile copy shall be considered binding and sufficient in the same manner as an original.

[Agreement to be signed by all of those in attendance at mediation.]

APPENDIX B

SELECTED BIBLIOGRAPHY

Negotiation

Fisher, R and Brown, S, *Getting Together: Building Relationships as We Negotiate*, 1991, New York: Penguin Books

Fisher, R and Ertel, D, *Getting Ready to Negotiate: The Getting to Yes Workbook*, 1995, New York: Penguin Books

Fisher, R, Kopelman, E and Kupfer Schneider, A, *Beyond Machiavelli: Tools for Coping with Conflict*, 1995, New York: Penguin Books

Fisher, R, Ury, W and Patton, B, *Getting to Yes: Negotiating Agreement Without Giving In*, 2nd edn, 1991, New York: Penguin Books

Gifford, DG, *Legal Negotiation, Theory and Applications*, 1989, St Paul: West Publishing Co

Hall, L (ed), *Negotiation, Strategies for Mutual Gain*, 1993, Newbury Park, CA: SAGE Publications, Inc

Lax, DA and Sebenius, J, *The Manager as Negotiator: Bargaining for Co-operation and Competitive Gain*, 1986, New York: The Free Press

Mnookin, R, Peppet, S and Tulumello, A, *Beyond Winning*, 2000, Cambridge, Mass: Harvard UP

Raiffa, H, *The Art and Science of Negotiation*, 1982, Cambridge, Mass: Harvard UP

Ury, W, *Getting Past No: Negotiating Your Way from Confrontation to Co-operation*, 1991, New York: Bantam Books

Watkins, M, *Breakthrough Business Negotiation*, 2002, San Francisco, CA: Jossey-Bass

Williams, G, *Legal Negotiation and Settlement*, 1983, Minneapolis, MN: West Publishing

Mediation

Brett, J, Drieghe, R and Shapiro, D, 'Mediator style and mediation effectiveness' (1986) 2 Negotiation J 277

Burke, JE and Boyle, PJ, 'Most successful mediators are masters of negotiation' (2000) 223 (103) NY Law Journal 9

Bush, RAB and Folger, J, *The Promise of Mediation: Responding to Conflict Through Empowerment and Recognition*, 1994, San Francisco, CA: Jossey-Bass

Davis, AM and Salem, RA, 'Dealing with power imbalances in the mediation of interpersonal disputes' (1984) 6 Mediation Q 17

Deitz, RM, 'Mediate with an expert: contrary to perceived role, they are catalysts for resolution' (2000) 223(122) NY Law Journal 56

Domenici, K and Littlejohn, SW, *Mediation: Empowerment in Conflict Management*, 1996, Long Grove, IL: Waveland Press, Inc

Emond, DP (ed), *Commercial Dispute Resolution: Alternatives to Litigation*, 1989, Aurora, ON: Canada Law Book Inc

Goldberg, SB, Sander, FEA and Rogers, NH, *Dispute Resolution: Negotiation, Mediation and Other Processes*, 1992, Toronto: Little Brown & Co

Green, ED, 'Corporate alternative dispute resolution' (1986) 1 Ohio State J on Disp Resol 203

Hermann, M and Bennett, MD, *The Art of Mediation*, 1996, South Bend, IN: The National Institute for Trial Advocacy

Honeyman, C, 'Bias and mediators' ethics' (1986) 2 Negotiation J 175

Kolb, DM, 'Labor mediators, managers, and ombudsmen: roles mediators play in different contexts', in Kressel K and Pruitt, D (eds), *Mediation Research: The Process and Effectiveness of Third Party Intervention*, 1996, San Francisco, CA: Jossey-Bass

Moore, C, *The Mediation Process: Practical Strategies for Resolving Conflict*, 2nd edn, 1996, San Fancisco, CA: Jossey-Bass

Noble, C, Dizgun, LL and Emond, DP, *Mediation Advocacy: Effective Client Representation in Mediation Proceedings*, 1998, Toronto: Emond Montgomery Publications

Roberts, M, 'Who is in charge? – reflections on recent research on the role of the mediator' (1992) J Social Welfare & Fam L 372

Roth, BJ, Wulff, RW and Cooper, CA (eds), *The Alternative Dispute Resolution Practice Guide*, 1999, Danvers: West Group

Seul, JR, 'How transformative is transformative mediation?: a constructive-developmental assessment' (1999) 15 Ohio State J On Disp Resol 135

Shapiro, D, Drieghe, R and Brett, J, 'Mediator behaviour and the outcome of mediation' (1995) 41 J Social Issues 101

Singer, LR, *Settling Disputes: Conflict Resolution in Business, Families, and the Legal System*, 1990, Boulder, CO: Westview Press, Inc

Stark, J, 'The ethics of mediation evaluation: some troublesome questions and tentative proposals, from an evaluative lawyer mediator' (1997) 38 South Texas Law Rev 769

Stitt, AJ, *Alternative Dispute Resolution For Organisations: How to Design a System for Effective Conflict Resolution*, 1998, Toronto: John Wiley & Sons, Canada

Stitt, AJ (ed), *Alternative Dispute Resolution Practice Manual*, updated annually, Toronto: CCH Canadian

INDEX